Four Years

A Navy Medic's
World War II Memories

Written by
H.C. Goldsmith

With His Grandson, Adam Gellert

Cypress River Publishing

Other Printings
ISBN: 978-0-595-47697-8 (pbk)
ISBN: 978-0-595-91960-4 (ebk)
iUniverse

Printed in the United States of America

Cypress River Publishing

Contents

Introduction 5

Four Years 1941-1945 9

    War Begins 10

    USS Sentinel 11

    To Africa 13

    Gibraltar and Straits 15

    Tenes, Algeria 17

    Oran, Algeria 18

    First Air Raid 20

    Navy Life in Oran 21

    Bizerte, Tunisia 25

    July 4, 1943 36

    July 5, 1943 36

    Invasion of Sicily 38

    "The Rains"—The *Sentinel* Sinks 41

    Waiting to Go Home 51

    Puerto Rico 54

    Trinidad, British West Indies 56

    Back to the Atlantic—USS Oswald 58

    War Ends 65

Epilogue—*Sentinel* Reunion 69

About the Authors 75

Introduction

The year 2000 was a great year for my grandfather. He turned 90 on March 25th. He was able to reunite with some of his shipmates from the U.S.S. Sentinel after almost 60 years (more about the reunion in the epilogue). He saw his first grandson get married in June. Finally, he witnessed another grandson get commissioned into the Navy, and even better, being assigned to a minesweeper as he was.

But it was also the year he died. On September 30th, I received a call from my mother to come quickly to Dallas. It was the worst day of my life to that point, never really having lost someone as close to me as my grandfather was. I like to think that God, knowing that the end was near, tried to pack as many wonderful things into his last year as He could.

One thing that immediately hit me when he died was the regret that I had never recorded Grandpa's World War II stories, either in a journal or by videotape. I grew up listening to his many stories of travels to Africa, Gibraltar, and Puerto Rico, and most importantly of the invasion of Sicily. I relived his horrific story of his ship being bombed, his friends dead or wounded, and Grandpa trying to save them all, since he was the ship's medic.

But then I received a wonderful gift. Sorting through his possessions, trying to figure out what to keep and what to throw away, hidden among his boxes of keepsakes, were three spiral-bound notebooks. Written in 1965, it was his account of his experiences during the War. I couldn't believe how fortunate I was to find his firsthand accounts, and I knew immediately that I had to transfer his journals to a computer for safekeeping. I also decided to make this journal into a book, to preserve his story and share it with others.

I finally completed transcribing his journals in September 2007, seven years after Grandpa's death. Why did it take so long? Because every word typed was like having him sitting there again, telling me his stories from his recliner, where he sat day in and day out watching TV. Seeing his handwriting, "listening" to his stories again, was sometimes too much. Many tears were shed while transcribing his journal, and I sometimes waited a year or more to open his notebook up and continue the project. This project was truly a labor of love, knowing that in the end the emotional journey it would take me on would be worth it.

The journal you are about to read, which my grandfather titled, "Four Years," confirms many of the stories he told me over the years. But it is an additional treasure because many of the stories were new to me, maybe forgotten over the years, maybe needing to be forgotten.

In his last years, Grandpa seemed to recall his war days more frequently. For someone I never saw cry, he cried frequently when mentioning his Sentinel shipmates, those "young boys" who died, some in his arms. As I compiled his story, the emotions of those days came alive, and I can see how war is both horrible and incredible at the same time. It must have been amazing to fear for your life, while at the same time bearing witness to the unbelievable display of sights and sounds all around you. Being a farm boy from Lewisville, Texas, it had to be quite an adventure to travel the world, wondering if you will ever see home again.

I have included a photo in this book of my grandfather holding me as a baby in 1974. That was the beginning of a special and unique relationship. I never got tired of spending time with Grandpa, and I loved listening to his war stories most of all. My mother thinks we were soul mates, and I believe that. I dream of him often and wish he could be here to see this book—he never told me about this journal and probably forgot that he had written it.

My grandfather is buried in Arlington National Cemetery in Washington, D.C. His wife, Byrdeen, died in 2007 and is buried with him. It is only fitting that he is with so many heroes of our nation who fought in our country's wars.

When I originally published this book in 2007, right after my grandmother died, I mentioned that my wife was pregnant with Grandpa's first great-grandson. Now, ten years later, he has almost a dozen great-grandkids who will get to read this story and know what their great-grandfather, along with so many other men and women of his generation, did to serve their country in a unique time in history.

I know Grandpa would be excited to share this story with all of you, as he did so often with me. And let's remember those who weren't able to return to tell their unique story of bravery and courage…

—Adam Gellert

GRANDPA AND ME, 1974

GRANDPA WITH ME AND HIS FAVORITE CHAIR

Four Years 1941-1945

This compilation of memories, started during World War II, was inspired by my wife (Byrdeen) and children (Linda & Betty) on this day, January 7, 1965. It is based on notes written during my time in service, as well as those recalled after 20 years, which are never very far from my mind.

GRANDPA WITH WIFE BYRDEEN, MY MOM BETTY (BOTTOM LEFT) AND LINDA, 1960.

War Begins

December 7, 1941—Sunday afternoon—attack on USA installations in Hawaiian Islands by Japan Imperial Forces.

Just prior to this date, from October 3, 1929 to September 13, 1933, my first tour of duty in the US Navy began and ended. On January 8, 1934, my employment started at Ford Motor Company, 5200 E. Grand, Dallas.

December 8, 1941 at 11 a.m., the late President Roosevelt asked and got, a Declaration of War against the then Axis Powers. This speech, before both houses of Congress, was heard at the Ford Plant Drug Store on my lunch period. My immediate reaction was "this is my war too," and having had previous military training, my little help was needed at once.

Upon returning to work, after lunch, this was expressed to my boss. Since my work hours permitted getting off duty early in the afternoons, my presence was made at the Recruiting Office in the Post Office on Ervay Street to get "lined up" for enlistment. For several days, my help was used in the Medical Department with Dr. Herndan Little and Chief Williams before my swearing in on December 13, 1941. The old uniform was used again.

Captain W.B. Cranston, USN, swore me in. A twist of fate concerns Captain Cranston and me. In 1929, he swore me into the Navy in Dallas (on Commerce Street) and in 1933 the very same man signed my discharge papers on "Goat Island" Receiving Station in San Francisco, California. And here, this man "took me in again." My enlistment was for four years or War's duration. A military leave of absence was secured from Ford Motor Company.

Many thought the War would be of short duration. Maybe a few months. My Dad was one of the many who thought so. He became disturbed when a four-year enlistment was signed. The duration of my service turned out to be only a few months short of four years.

My verbal agreement with Captain Cranston was that my duties would be at the Recruiting Station for a while because of my sudden enlistment and in needing a chance to straighten my business before going to sea. My tour of duty at the Recruiting Station did extend until October 1942, when my transfer came for "New Construction" and sea duty.

While at the Recruiting Station in Dallas, the "Sea Bees" were born. Also, "Chief Specialists" came into being. These were the people who were to head the physical aspects of Navy training. Mr. Gene Tunney, ex-heavyweight boxing champion, paid us a visit. On our stretch of days, my duties required me to work 90 consecutive days, 16 hours per day, examining men for active duty. For this a Commendation of Loyalty to Duty was received. Some days four or five hundred men would be processed and shipped to boot camps.

U.S.S. Sentinel

Orders received and I departed on October 3, 1942, for duty aboard the *USS Sentinel* #113 in Lorain, Ohio, which was near completion. This city is west of Cleveland some 30 miles on Lake Erie. There were four of this type of ship being constructed in Lorain and four in Cleveland. They were "sister" ships and of the AM Class (Auxiliary Minesweeper). Two engine rooms of two engines each (diesel electric), twin screws, and the most powerful and largest of Minesweepers. Also the heaviest armored. It could serve as a tug they were so powerful. Many 20mm guns, two each of 3-inch guns, over 600 cans of TNT for both K-guns and to drop over the stern for submarine destroying. All of the eight sister ships' names started with an "S" (letter). Our compliment of men was 99 to 112.

U.S.S. Sentinel, under construction (Government Photo)

While in Lorain, the crew resided in private homes until ready to board the ships. The trial runs and dock trials were done in late November 1942. "Shade-down" trials were made on Lake Erie. When ships were ok'd, the ships' yard workmen took up a collection of over $300 for our ship's canteen. This was my responsibility, being Canteen Keeper along with the medical duties. Also, $20 extra monthly pay. This ship's store was non-profit.

About November 11, 1942, the four ships at Lorain went up to Cleveland and headed down the Saint Lawrence River for the open sea. Twenty-seven locks were necessary to go through on the way to the Atlantic Ocean. On one of the river curves and rapids, we went aground.

One screw (we had two screws) was bent. Spent 3-4 days in Montreal dry docked for repairs. At Quebec, a terrific storm was encountered. Couldn't tie up at dock. Had to stay in bay. After leaving Quebec for Boston and near Prince Edward Island, the ship listed (in a storm) several times to a 44-46 degree. The ship was constructed to take a 76-degree list.

Arrived at Boston shipyards on the Charles River about December 12, 1942. Since these ships were started and almost completed before wartime, a lot of construction that could burn was removed from the ship. Also, the latest radar, de-gauging, and sonar equipment was installed. The crew stayed at Frazier Barracks on the shipyard grounds. The ship "Old Ironsides" was tied up near us.

During these few days in Boston and near Christmas, it was cold. 40 degrees below zero one time. A few blocks from our shipyard, the "Coconut Grove" night club burned, along with 300-400 people. Christmas decorations caught fire and added to make it very bad and costly. The mayor of Boston ordered all decorations in the city removed.

After some two months in Boston Navy shipyards, we were ready for trial runs again and target practice off Portland, Maine (Casco Bay). Submarine tracking practice was done at the New London, Connecticut sub base. Here is where "White Christmas" was first heard.

Our first sea duty, seeking the enemy, was off Cape Hatteras, North and South Carolina. This was the area where Axis subs were sinking a lot of ships. We and one other ship traversed an area of some 50 miles long, back and forth, for two weeks (in sight of land). No subs were encountered on this patrol. A large whale, thought to be one, was disturbed by our depth charges, for it surfaced, "blew" his top, and went merrily on its way. Maybe we were trigger happy. We then returned to New York and Brooklyn Navy Yard. Here we received a good check and loaded all necessary supplies for overseas duty.

To Africa

About April 1, 1943, we departed from Brooklyn Navy Yard, under the Brooklyn Bridge, down the East River, past the Lady of Freedom, "The Statue of Liberty" and out past Ambrose Lighthouse to the open sea. Then we first knew our destination—Africa.

The invasion of Africa had been made on November 12, 1942, on the west coast of North Africa and south of the "Rock of Gibraltar". A large amount of supplies and fresh troops were needed. So as one of the armed escorts, we were assigned to protect a convoy across the Atlantic. In any ocean crossing, all warships are used to escort convoys, even when needed to be used in the war zone. Our ship was of these types and was to remain in the Mediterranean Sea for duty.

This early morning when we were leaving New York harbor, the "Lady" and lower Manhattan Island grew dim and faded away behind us. After passing Ambrose Light Ship at the entrance to New York Harbor, some of the escorts were milling around and others were coming behind us. This was a very slow convoy of about 8 knots (9 miles an hour). Traveling 9 miles per hour and over 3,000 miles to go. There were all types and sizes of the smaller warships. This meant a slow journey and an easy sub target. To name a few, destroyers, LST, liberty vessels, SC, LSM, tankers, and tugs. There were no passenger ships of any kind. Just the slow, heavy-laden cargo types. About 33 warships formed the protection and were all around the precious cargo ships with supplies our boys needed. Many liberty ships had all kinds of broken down airplanes on the top deck and many railroad cars and engines of the narrow-gauge type used in the lands we were headed for. Other than fighting ships, the ships being escorted numbered 100. This meant that when all cargo ships were lined up in lines of about 10 each, with the escorts around them (to the sides, front, and back), one could hardly see the lead ship.

Our station was the very last ship at the end of the convoy. This also meant that for any ship having engine trouble, it was our duty to stay with it; the others never slowed. Our ship did drop back and stay with one LST for two days. Engine trouble, and while being repaired, we just kept circling the LST until she got under way. The other ships were out of sight, and there were no tracks or markings on the ocean. About the fourth day, the Sentinel and LST rejoined the convoy, and that feeling of a sub watching from behind every second was relieved.

Bermuda, the isle of beauty. We put into the Port of Hamilton for one day. The climate is wonderful. The water a hue of blue all its own. The coral was beautiful and was fished for. When hooked and brought to the surface, one only had to boil the fish to preserve it. Otherwise, the odor was terrific. Seems all the houses were of a different color except the roof of white seashells. One might say tropical with a British accent. The USA had bases on many of these islands on a 99-year lease for the War I type destroyers traded for this right.

Many more ships were collected upon leaving Bermuda. Some British joined the convoy. Into the rising sun we proceeded. Some 11 days had passed since Bermuda. Then came the traversing of "Torpedo Junction" near the Canary Islands. This is an area where ships come and go, in and out the straits of Gibraltar and on down the coast of Africa or to Western Europe, England, and west to the USA. Here, near the Canary Islands, part of our convoy broke off and headed for the west coast of Africa and Casablanca.

This crossing was a very uneventful one. The refueling of ships at sea was carried out by all ships at least once. Simply, a ship would go alongside a tanker, never stopping, when a line would be thrown over to the ship to be refueled, and a hose attached to receive oil. Like a mother feeding her baby—walking. Only, our ship got too close to the tanker and a swell in the ocean threw our sides together. Our gun turret caved in and a K-gun stand was knocked over and bent. A lot of noise, but a great change for something different to happen. No sight or sound of the enemy during the entire crossing. The sighting of the "Rock" was a relief and a haven of safety. We had passed a spot where many ships had been torpedoed, especially during prior years of the war. The German subs operated here near Gibraltar Straits (a crossroads) since September 1939. Now, in 1943, air cover was available. The fighters would range far out to sea and then come back to meet us. A plane can see the dark color of a sub far under the water. This is why subs come nearer the surface at times very near sunset and sunrise for their attack.

Gibraltar and Straits

The cargo ships of our convoy entered the Strait, through the submarine nets and into the harbor in a single line—like follow the leader in a zig-zag course. The escort or warships just peeled back and entered the harbor last. Near late evening all were nestled in the harbor. The Straits are about 8 miles wide and 30 miles long. This is the waterway connection between the Mediterranean Sea and the Atlantic Ocean. Africa to the south and Western Europe to the north. There is very little tide movement in the Sea, which drains to the Atlantic. The Rock is some 2000 feet high. On its south and west sides are large concrete slabs covering most of it, which drains the rainfall for storage. It's the only source of fresh water. This "Rock" is called the best and most heavily fortified spot in the world. England has controlled it for over 200 years. The harbor is so large it can hold all the world's navy ships at one time.

This one night we spent harbored here was a noisy one. The enemy would use divers to float mines which were attached to a ship's screw. When the screw moved, the mine would explode. These mines and divers came from the Spanish mainland under the cover of night. To overcome this, during the night, at regular intervals, a British corvette would go its rounds, dropping depth charges which would explode any mine in the water, hoping to do this before being attached to a vessel's screw. This one night stand was April 23, 1943.

The Mediterranean Sea as a beautiful sight to behold. Still another hue of blue all its own. It was spring. As we proceeded up the north coast of Africa, going east, the countryside was lovely to see. We were nearing the enemy and the land where fighting was in progress.

The first sight of the enemy was sighted on April 25, 1943. But he was quite harmless. It was the floating body of a Nazi aviator. His yellow parachute pack showed above water. Before this pack was identified, the all-stations alarm was sounded. It was reported by a lookout that a periscope was sighted. When the sun was made toward it, it was then discovered not being a sub periscope but the floating aviator. After circling him, the skipper (Mr. Phillips) decided not to pick up the body, so we rejoined the convoy. Being the only medical man aboard, my job would have been to take care of the details. My presence on top deck was for this purpose.

As we cruised up the coast of Africa, Oran, Algeria, came into view. Ships from our convoy peeled out of their formation and headed into Oran. Only 4 escorts and 8 merchant ships remained in the original group. We headed up the coast to Tenes, Algeria. Arrived there after 26 days' sailing.

Tenes, Algeria

This was a small town, some 1000-1200 people. Had the usual wall around the city. City square with a little park and a church. The city had not been damaged except one thing noticeably. That was the church steeple. All the church steeples were very high for the size of the building. The upper or topmost part of the steeple was missing. Ask why and how come? The Germans were using it for observation and pinpointing their artillery fire. So, we first shot the top off and that ended the evil eye.

Liberty was granted in the war zone from 3 p.m. until sunset. The harbors of all their cities had masonry-constructed break water and always facing the open sea. To enter the harbor, a ship had to go around and sort of behind to the entrance. The pier accommodated about 2-3 ships. Our ship was the only one there. All others went in to a little town back west toward Oran.

All new ships, such as ours, were given a complete set of sports equipment when commissioned. So that very afternoon, a softball game was played near our ship. All hands had to play ball and it was the first time we had been on land in almost a month. My job was to see to the health of the crew and this exercise was easy.

The shoreline was rugged and hilly. Lots of greenery and very pretty weather. About 200-300 yards from our ship lay a German plane pretty well stripped. It was a photo plane. When shot down, the latest photography equipment was aboard. It was stripped and sent to the States. You see, the armies were fighting just inland and toward the east of us. We could hear the guns. At this time, our ship was farthest east of any, and nearest the land fighting. Well, this plane was shot down by a sub chaser's cook the day before we arrived. He had cooked the noon meal and was standing gun watch while the 10 or 11 crewmen were eating. This plane circled a couple of times near him when he saw the swastika marking and proceeded to shoot it down. We were told he just pointed the gun (probably a 20 mm) at it and shot the thing down. Besides, he says, it was bothering my rest and reading.

A lot of the people in the city could speak English. There were a lot of shortages. Especially chew gum, soap, cigarettes, etc. You see, they were cut off from France (French-Algeria) and had been in the war for some four years then. All of the locals were ragged and very dirty. The children seemed to suffer most. One little boy, eight years old, always met me when leaving the ship to go ashore. The first time his reward was a stick of gum. Dozens of kids in the group always latched onto the first sailor who gave them something.

"My" little boy was dirty and diseased. Most all his hair was gone from ringworm or some other disease. Sores all over his face and hands. Had infected eyes. This kid, as most of them, was a beggar. When given anything, and the eyes were taken off him, he would not have it in his hand when looking back at him. Only his right hand could be seen. He wore a cloak or a large piece of cloth as a cloak, only tied at the neck. Never could catch him disposing of objects given him. Finally, his cloak was jerked back off and from over his left side and arm (if there was one). He had a left arm about the size as when he was a one year old. A small half-gallon bucket, with a bail, was hanging from the head of his elbow. The arm had never been used except to carry this bucket on his rounds of begging. In this bucket was found cigarette butts, tinfoil, matches, etc.

These people had plenty of money. Just nothing to spend it on. Our skipper had to stop our crew from selling pillow cases, mattress covers, etc. to the natives. They had plenty of French Francs. When, for instance, a mattress cover was sold for $5 and up, the buyer would cut three holes in one end (the sewn end) and put his hand and arms through and wear it. One native had on five at one time.

Oran, Algeria

After some five days in Tenes, we were ordered to Oran about 100 miles back to the west, where we had passed days before. The weather was beautiful and the sea like glass. Lots of greenery, flowers, and fruit tree blooms over the rolling hills along the shoreline. Oran's harbor was of the same appearance as the others, with a break water wall and gate to enter. This was a city of some 200,000 people. High mountains were to the west of the harbor, while the rolling hill (the city) was to the south. It was a very large harbor. This was the base for the French Mediterranean Fleet. Only most all of the fleet was sunk here, or at least scuttled. The French were quite divided. The "Vickey" French were pro-Nazi, but the "Free" French were pro-Allies. The "Free" French scuttled these ships rather than surrender after our Casablanca invasion and our push through the city toward the east.

The city was under martial law. Damaged and sunken ships of all types and sizes were all over the harbor. Some were burned out while at anchor. Others broken in half. Some on sides, and some smaller with the funnels above water. One was a large passenger vessel on its side. The water was from 40 feet deep in the channel to 25 feet out toward the sea walls. Some had been re-floated and some being re-floated for repair. Five subs had been sunk by the French. Two were in the dry dock and being repaired.

The activity was tremendous. Many ships were being hurriedly unloaded of the supplies of war so that another trip could be made to America for more of the same. From one area of docks, guns, planes, locomotives, tanks, food, drums of oil and gasoline, and ammo were being unloaded. This was our largest and closest port to the fighting front.

The city itself was beautiful. The buildings well-constructed. All floors, in any height building, had beautiful tile floors. Plenty of parks, well kept, and very nice beaches. My first bikini bathing suit was seen on the beach here. Also saw one with a top that was made of a US Navy pillowcase. The boy's name was on one and another said "Navy" on it. The people had plenty to eat, lots of money, plenty of fruits and vegetables. The streets were narrow and so were the sidewalks. Running water was at the curb on many streets for washing and soaking feet. Restrooms were on the sidewalk with only a swinging door to enter. One's feet and head could be seen. Many Nazi collaborators were still in the city. Many service men of all branches were slain for their shoes, etc.

First Air Raid

For three to four days we had enjoyed the shore leave (3 pm until sunset) and visits about the city. We always traveled in groups when ashore. The fighting was some 640 miles to the east of us and fast coming to a close in the Northwest Africa theater of war. Each morning at daybreak and each evening at sunset, all hands manned their battle stations. Most enemy planes came in at one of these times. On the evening of May 8, 1943, at 2100, the bombers came in. The cliffs and hills around the harbor afforded them protection from radar. They were on us without warning. The first bomb brought me out of my sack with little or no effort. The call to battle stations had been released. They came in much later—after dark. My first view on top side, just outside my battle dressing station, was something to behold. The surrounding land guns (Army) and the ships' guns were all blasting away up into the dark. The Army defense played their search lights into the sky. The tracer shells from the smaller caliber guns almost lighted the darkness. With the larger guns, from 6-inch and up, one could follow the projectile for yards after penetrating the night. The noise and "boom, boom" of the larger guns was deafening. A stick of three bombs straddled our ship. Two of them only raised a geyser of water—the third hit the fan-tail of a liberty ship near us. The liberty ship was at the very spot, unloading, where we were berthed the day before. Our ship was moved to make way for them. The bomb hit on top of the gun crew, killing all five, and a fire burned furiously.

The British ships always left any enclosed harbor when attacked. This was because of the narrow entrances to the harbor which could be blocked by the sinking of one ship in its mouth. They were cagey, good fighters and loved a challenge.

One bomb hit a newly-built building used for toilets on the beach across from us. Three soldiers took refuge in this building at the onset of the attack and were killed. Most all merchant ships at this stage of the war had installed guns on them. Navy crews manned the guns. The alert and fireworks lasted 45 minutes. Our only casualty was a mashed left hand at the 4th-5th fingers. This man (name forgotten) was loading the forward 3-inch gun when the breach was closed on his hand. Left hand held the 3-inch shell and the right hand was used to push the shell into the gun. With special permission and a lot of details this man was taken to the Army base hospital in the city of Oran. This was quite an experience and kind of spooky, being 11 o'clock at night and the city in a complete blackout.

Also, the Coxswain went into hysteria during the attack. He was one of the two 3-inch gun captains. A hard draw back and slap across the cheek quieted him down. One other time this man did the same thing and the same treatment cured him. He never remembered either instance.

There are no atheists in battles. If anyone ever said he wasn't scared, he's either crazy or a liar. To my knowledge, we downed two bombers. The ships in the harbor got one and an Army private with a 30 caliber, water-cooled machine gun got the other. This private was stationed on the outer perimeter of the defense and when the plane came in low, hedge hopping, he let him have it. This was learned upon my trip the next day when visiting and checking my man with the injured hand at the base hospital. Some of the boys said this private simply went berserk and ran in circles yelling, "I got him" over and over until he was caught and restrained. This private's gun position was near a cemetery and several "pup" tents housed each gun crew. Bombs unearthed several graves. One bomb hit one of these tent areas and all four of its members were reported killed. There were only three deaths, for one of the four was A.W.O.L.

The German radio, "Axis Sally" gave reports of devastating damage in the harbor and elsewhere. Not true in the harbor area for sure. We tuned in to Axis Sally most of the time. The music was better than ours or the BBC from London. Their radio news also gave more detail of the overall war picture.

Navy Life in Oran

One afternoon a couple of us were sitting on the fan-tail sunning when one boy asked us to help him investigate a bunch of kegs on the sea bottom. So, Bullock (from Weatherford, Texas) undressed, dived down, hooked a rope or line around one of the flasks, and with the use of a hand-cranked crane, up it came. We were all elated when we found it full of rare wine. About this time the Skipper, who had been watching us from the ship's bridge, proceeded to have it shoved back overboard into its watery grave. Well, he wasn't very popular after that.

Life aboard the ship, the daily routine, the tension present every moment, was at times hard to endure. The chow was, at times, hard to eat much less smell. Dry rations, powdered this and that, dehydrated this and that, canned this and that, didn't keep morale very high. Differences among shipmates arose. Nerves strained and arguments, personal and state wise arose. Most personal differences were settled with the boxing gloves. Some were had out before the gloves could be tied on.

All ship portholes were sealed for the duration. All lights in any one compartment were wired so when one would enter or leave through the door, the lights would be shut off. The mess hall was also the "Rec Room". "Old Oscar" the fresh water maker seemed to be always out of order. Some thought the man who cared for it just didn't. The one automatic, open-ended clothes washer always needed repair. Blankets and mattresses always needed airing on top side, and from the stench, these were never aired enough. This boy Bullock (Big Tex) was my checker opponent. Sometimes our games, won and lost between us, would be in the hundreds. Any game unfinished at day's end was completed on the tomorrow or hours following.

Broken or interrupted rest was never accustomed to. Long and regular sleep was unheard of. My bunk was in the forward crew quarters, the top most of three bunks in a tier. The sick bay was near me. All crew members knew my location day or night. Duties for the "Doc" were on a 24-hour basis. While in port, any time in my absence, a "Doc" from a nearby ship was on call. Supplies of some kinds were scarce. The Navy had no supply depots in this area. The Army ran this theater area and medical supplies were requisitioned or begged from them. Not too much trouble, for one could always find a "Texan" to help a friend in need. Some four Texans were aboard and yet they weren't any closer to me than Ted Oie from San Francisco. He was the Storekeeper and we shared the same typewriter, office, etc. We were fortunate to make trips together for supplies. All food that went through his work the Doc inspected. The Canteen supplies, that is, cigarettes, soap, etc., was my charge. Needed re-supplying a lot and nice trips ashore and even inland were made (more later on Ted Oie).

The Yeoman named Tom Batson, from Dallas, Texas, was our close shipmate. We were what one might call "white collar" workers. He cared for all the ship's records, except medical, and the Captain's correspondence. Yes, at times the Texans, New Jersey, and Brooklyn boys would clash but most always in a friendly manner. This one old boy who let his whiskers grow since leaving the States was really put out. Since a boy's whiskers, on a sister ship, caught fire, we all had to shave often. Mine was a "Van Dyke." There were quite a variety of designs among the crew members.

The ships that unloaded and headed home for more supplies didn't help morale much. Everyone envied them. Still, they brought fresh food, mail, etc. Yes, mail. Sometimes the news helped, sometimes it hurt. Some boys lost loved ones. Some lost a wife at home. The huge cargo net unloading thousands and thousands of bags of mail were always welcomed. At one time a box of cigars, chewing tobacco, etc. was delivered to me after being re-wrapped three times, made the rounds of the Pacific theater of war, and finally to North Africa. Took some 12 months. Letters came two days old, together with two-month old letters. Since the "Doc" had grain alcohol for medicinal purposes, the cook could always need some when a chocolate pie was found near or in sick bay. So, at times morale could never have been higher.

After about three more days in Oran and during that time keeping up with the War's progress, we headed east. We were one of three escorts for the first convoy for Bizerte, Tunisia, 640 miles away. The War in Northwest Africa had ceased. The enemy, the Rommel Africa Corps, surrendered at Bizerte on May 9th and Cape Bon, Tunisia on the 12th of May, 1943. That is, the land resistance ceased. Not the air war.

After four days sailing east and upon passing the cities of Phillipville and Bone, we, while at sea, watched the night bombing of the cities we had occupied after pushing through them and building up supplies there. Appeared as a show for us. War is fascinating at times, a simply beautiful sight to behold. Also, we were winning just as in a sports contest. All plays look good when winning. We were now some 40-50 miles from Bizerte and were not disturbed.

Sailing on the placid Mediterranean Sea is quite an experience. No body of water is so beautiful. Even the shorelines, the sunsets, and sunrise are something to see. A cruise here, in peacetime, must be one of a lifetime.

From the very beginning of our duty aboard the Sentinel, special gear was issued. The regulation helmet with lines, "Mae West" life jacket, and gas mask. These three items were carried with us at all times. In fact, at night, they were our bedmates. The threat of gas was ever present. The rumors of the enemy dropping, shooting, etc., of these poisonous gases were constantly passed around. Especially when the enemy was pushed into any corner. One could see the tide had turned or was turning in our favor. Through desperation, many thought the Axis Powers would try anything.

This one night, we were about 12 miles from shore (on water, distance seems nearer), and the big moon looked down from above. A calm sea made subs more likely to attack. In the heavens, bombers were more apt to strike. The planes were probably coming from Sicily and Italy. They came in droves, somewhat spaced. They always came in from the land side. This meant they circled around, coming from the east going south and then back over us toward the sea to the north and east. There were flashes of bomb bursts, fire, and smoke. There were many guns at sea and land firing tracers that streaked the sky in long, frilly lines described like the blood vessels in one's arm. Moments of quietness and then the fury of war again.

Of course, during these few days it wasn't the enemy doing all the "punching." Day and night, our bombers, B-17 and B-24, would head to the east and north, coming over us at sea, from our advance bases in this Northwest Africa theater. Many times, we would count the bombers going out and then count them coming back home. Most always, the figure was less than the original. The round-trip for our boys was about

200-300 miles. Most trips, fighter (P-38 and P-40) protection was given. Even convoys had fighter protection when in their range. Constantly, fighters were near our ship, down low near the water, looking for subs. The color of the water afforded sighting a sub quite deep. Subs in the Mediterranean Sea were never a great threat. At first, the subs would be on the bottom, near shore, and attack at night. The planes would fly low and very near shore seeking any shadow or the ribbon of bubbles from their screws. It was fun when one would be spied. In moments, several planes would converge on it like food in a chicken yard when one hen found it. These young fighter pilots of ours were so very daring. Life must have been short for a lot. Almost hit our "Crow's Nest" just playing and diving on us. Nevertheless, their presence made one feel a little more secure. It was a team effort and their part was played well.

Something that stands out was the enemy bombers coming so near our ship and convoy in the moonlit night. They would be heading for home now, and were very near the water. Their motors were very noisy, like being right on top of us. How they missed our ships, I don't know. We had orders not to shoot, since they might not know we were there. Any shooting they would know. You see, in our convoy was one especially important ship. It was a Liberty ship with specially trained divers and demolition crew aboard. They were to help clear the harbor and debris at Bizerte.

Bizerte, Tunisia

The city of Bizerte was a pre-war city of some 20,000. She came into view behind a point of land which stuck out into the sea. This point of land was the northern-most point of the continent of Africa. The city was only 15 feet above sea level. The land sloped back inland to a mountain backdrop. This was May 17, 1943, when we circled to enter the channel to the harbor. We were told for three months of the year the harbor was unusable because of the severe dust storms blowing from the desert only 40-60 miles to the south. The cargo vessels were anchored outside the main harbor. The British minesweepers were all busy sweeping mines. Smaller ships, as ours, could enter the entrance to the harbor. There were many damaged and sunken ships. Some 15 were counted of sizes and types. Tugs, divers, TNT, etc., were making headway clearing the entire channel. Within 4-5 days, this enemy-blocked channel was being used. Lake Bizerte lay 2-3 miles inland from the Sea through this channel.

This was the first American convoy here. You see, the British were already there, for only a few miles away to the east and south lay Malta. She had been bombed about every day since the War started three years before. This island fortress afforded a great thorn in the Axis' side. Meaning, she never quite controlled the Sea. Finally, an ally, a friend had arrived and the Allies now controlled the Sea.

This channel afforded a very constant danger. For at the bottom of the channel lay mines the Axis left that would explode after so many ships went over them. Some were set at three, four, five, 25, etc. passes. Any time of the day, a great explosion could be heard and another ship crippled or damaged. Along the channel and Lake Bizerte shores, land mines could be heard and seen when an unfortunate local would come to bathe or just sit and watch. Fast as could be, areas were being cleared of mines and booby traps. The city lay flat where only weeks before it stood. The city was built right down to the sea shore and dock side. The streets were palm-lined. Only a sentry on guard could be seen ashore here and there. The stench or smell was terrific. Many enemy bodies lay buried in the crumpled buildings. Our artillery laid the city flat after the enemy was pushed to here. The Vickey, French, Italians, and Germans were here. Still, many signs of very familiar names could be seen. Standard Oil, Esso, Ford Motor Company, General Electric, etc. We were anchored in mid-stream nearer to the airport about 200 yards from either shore, and near my ship we saw our first submarine pen in a small hill at the channel shore.

This was May 18, 1943. This hill or cliff formed the sub pen and entrance from the shore and waterline. There were three sub entrances in a row, carved out of this stone-like substance. The top of this hill had two vents for the powerhouse and to exhaust fumes and get fresh air. Two of the three tunnel-like openings could be seen caved in from its opening. The enemy had done this before surrendering. They were never touched again. The air field was some 200 yards to the west. The concrete sea plane apron lay from the water to the building. There were 10 or 12 concrete hangars. All of them were badly damaged or destroyed but one. The Allies (here we had become blended with the British) were using this good hangar. The others had many French, Italian, and German planes in them. Several torpedoes, bombs, etc., lay about. This entire picture showed two powerful factories had met, struggled, and desolation was the result. The enemy destroyed some—but our artillery and planes did most of the destroying.

On May 19, 1943, my first trip was made ashore. My duties in charge of the Canteen called for supplies. Cigarettes were rationed. The Navy had set up a dispensary or field hospital, which was French, and then occupied by Germans, and now we were in it. Most all activities were carried on by the Army. Besides the lands cleared of rubble, were signs warning of booby traps, unexploded mines, etc. Some had a little fence around or to the side. We were constantly warned to chance nothing. Their booby traps were plentiful. Some were real-looking fountain pens. When the cap would be taken off an explosion resulted right into one's face. Some were cigarette lighters, fake helmets, and German war booty. They knew the Americans to be souvenir hunters and very inquisitive. Curiosity got the best of some during the war.

The mail clerk made this trip with me. At this early time of arrival, no mail had found us. Several trips were dry runs. The flies were in the majority and such pests. Small with red-like tail and never heard them. They would land and stick. Had to brush them off. They were always looking for moisture—this meant landing in the eye corner or mouth. The stink was again very bad. Their buildings in this part of the world were a lot of masonry, stacked. Steel support was scarce—fell a lot like dominoes.

Most every afternoon, and one could set his watch by him, "Ol' Photo Joe" came over. The German plane took its high-level pictures and knew just what we were doing. Sometimes one could see his vapor trail. Most times could see nothing. But it did cause a "Red Alert! Man battle stations." Very seldom was any firing ever done at him.

For the next four days, or until May 23, 1943, we did minesweeping. The ships coming and going were ever increasing in number. We would go out into the channel opening every morning and sweep for mines. At night, the enemy would "sow" mines by air or subs and we would have to go out and destroy them. The British did most of it. They had smaller wooden hull sweepers. These would not attract a certain kind of mine as a steel hull would. Believe me, they had plenty of experience.

One type of mine was like a ball which was anchored about 7-8 feet underwater. These exploded upon contact. A trigger or cap was on its surface. Our sweeping equipment was two floating "Paravanes" on cables. When under way, these were let out on a cable to either side of the ship's stern at about 100 yards. These cables (underwater to Paravane) had "cutters" or "scissors" along the cable's length. When the cable or chain anchoring the mine was hit, it was cut into at the scissor on the Paravane cable. It would float and on a return trip, would be exploded from a distance by our gun crews. Another type of mine we were after was the time mine. It would be set off at a given number of ships passing over it, and a certain number of screw (propeller) turns. A contraption of a "trip hammer" type would be let off over the bow at a depth of three feet. Several thousand times per minute this hammer tripped with a noisy thud. This set this type of mine off at a safe distance unless you started the hammer over one of these mines. Then it would be "Katy bar the door."

Even with this work and every precaution and warning for all ships to stay in a cleared channel, disaster would befall some. The life of a minesweeper was a short one. This duty carried us very near the small yet 1,000-foot-high island of Pantelleria. This island was enemy held and was about 20 miles from Cape Bon. Our planes bombed it into surrender. This island reminded me of a resort type. Very colorful homes on it and lots of greenery.

The trip of a lifetime for a sailor came my way on May 26, 1943. The Electrical Engineer, Storekeeper, and I requisitioned an Army truck to go inland 40 miles to Mateur, Tunisia. This took us across the battlefields of the late part of the war in North Africa. From the east came Montgomery pushing Rommel, and from the west came Patton pushing Nazi tallies ahead of him. Mateur was the important hub or junction and both sides must have this city.

We departed at 0800 from Bizerte for this main Army supply depot. If it wasn't for the Army, the Navy would have had nothing, yet this all came from the U.S. The Navy escorted it in cargo and Navy ships. Again, a team effort. Upon leaving the walled city of Bizerte, we passed this city of Kaulera, wherein was the airport. Here was the graveyard of many, maybe a thousand enemy planes, all destroyed. A lot of the Italian planes were of the WWI type. Near the hangers and ringing the port were many, ready to go, Allied fighter planes.

On the rolling hills, sloping to the mountains from the sea, is where over 200,000 war prisoners were dotting the landscape. These were mostly the Germans. The best they had, the Africa Corps. Rommel picked, one might say. Six-footers, blue eyed and blonde. From the sea, our first day in port, one could see these thousands of men on the hillsides, in wheat fields and watermelon patches. The War had ended for them. Many were doing Army chores, unloading ships, clearing streets, doing janitor work. Many spoke good English. All the Italian prisoners spoke of and were very anxious to go to America. The German prisoners were very afraid of raids. When we had the alert, the first, the enemy might be 5-10 miles away. They would not wait for the Red Alert and battle stations to see if they were coming. They would leave out from the dock area. They all thought, still, the Fuhrer reeked total destruction even from the air. They never admitted defeat in their hearts.

Near this city of Kaulera or this city within the walls, Bizerte, is where the song "Dirty Gertie from Bizerte" was written. The house where she was supposed to live with her mother was one with a two-foot-high picket fence around it.

The watermelons were ripe. They were about the size of our icebox melons and were very tasty. Most all kinds of fruits were here and there. The shoreline around Bizerte was sandy with scrub plants growing; seems it was cliff-like but not very high. The briers that "pipe bowls" are made of come principally from these shores. One can see literally thousands of these roots and nuts of the brier plant from the eroded embankment, which are said to be thousands of years old.

The highway leading and winding over the hills to Mateur was a narrow black top. All the bridges were destroyed either by our bombing ahead of the retreating enemy or their destroying behind their retreat. The holes in the bombed pavement were all filled in. Crops of many sorts were being harvested or cultivated. Many of our boys were helping them. When about 5 miles from the city, the people were living on the countryside after being driven from their houses. In this area, the enemy retreated rather rapidly and there were few signs of war.

Below Ferryville, about 5 miles away, lies Lake Ferryville, which is a salt lake below sea level. Then mountainous country. Near here is where the enemy made their last major resistance. The Second Army Corps split the Africa Corps of Rommel's just south of Ferryville which is at the south end of the salt lake and Bizerte.

Here, all the aftermath of war was evident. Brown splotches marked the grain fields. There were fox holes and bomb craters. All trees and groves had crisscrossing trenches and gun emplacements. Crashed planes, some burned, both ours and the enemy's, were here and there. Graves were nearly everywhere. Sometime alone and in other places two or three in a row. All had their gun or something sticking into the ground with their helmet on top. The enemy and our boys were sometimes together side by side. Many unspent and spent shells were near gun pits. Many tanks were here and there like monuments. Some with tracks off, some in scraps, showing direct hits, and others burned out. Graves were nearly always beside these tanks. Many burned haystacks were seen over the hillsides with the enemy guns and tanks in the ashes. One small American cub plane was seen straddling a fence. Looked undamaged.

Several small towns or villages were passed through which showed no war damage. Invariably, the fighting followed the valleys. When very near Mateur, hill 609 came into view. This is the hill the Germans offered such stiff resistance. It was at several valley junctions and the one who controlled it, held the way in several directions. Several hundred feet of this hill was literally blown off by bombs and artillery. This main hill opened the door to the coast through level ground. The hill did look flat-topped.

This city of Mateur looked like an anthill with valleys in all directions. A very commanding city to hold. A very important hub. This is the city that changed hands 5 times over several weeks' period. Easy to hold and hard to take. This city, the rubble, showed the effects of those see-saw battles. The cemetery or grave lots were visited. Soldiers of many nations and countries were buried here. The cross markings showed 1940-1943. Friend and foe buried side by side. The vegetation had grown over the area and how many acres in the cemetery could not be determined. Several acres were freshly planted with graves.

One thing we pointed to and discussed was the "eaten" away at the corners of buildings and at window ledges. Where men had stood and where some knelt at these positions was chipped away by bullets. Seemed every window, door, corner had these areas. Some places the ground was "paved" with empty shells of all makes. Late that evening, we returned with food, clothing (Army type), and medical supplies to Bizerte. One kind of medical item was grain alcohol. Never was there a cook, Army or Navy, who doesn't like a cup of "Coffee Royale." The need for this treatment was often for our cook when ingredients and end results of a good pie was found in the sick bay. Especially a double dose, for the nerves, when it was chocolate.

The Sentinel #113 received orders to proceed to Dellys, Algeria. This was back down the coast to the west near French Morocco and between Oran and Gibraltar. We pulled into Oran for one day, no mail yet. Almost 2 months and no news - except war news via radio. Our ship's yeoman put out a sheet of news almost every day. Reading between the lines helped. No mail is sent from the States until a ship's safe arrival and operational assignment had been established.

The Port of Oran had been cleared of a lot of the debris of war since our last visit. Many, many large transports and refrigeration ships were loading and unloading. After a visit on a large transport, seeking what one might call needed supplies, the gang plank guard held us up while about 1700 German prisoners went aboard. They were the best-looking soldiers ever seen. All seemed about the same size and healthy appearance. They were headed for America and Canada. This was the Africa Corps who fought the British in the desert for so long. We pulled into the Port of Dellys on the 5th or 6th of June 1943. This was the first visit of any allied ship in this port. All the townspeople must have met us. Very friendly were the natives. The city was like all others, walled in but very neat for what they had to make do with. Food was plentiful. They had no new clothes, cigarettes, soap, matches, etc. Some said the head of families offered their wives for service for scarce items. The purpose of this trip was never known unless for goodwill. Our stay was only 24 hours.

Finally, it became known our base of operations was Bizerte. On to the Port of Oran we proceeded. Oran was the main base coastwise and the traffic was terrific. We knew our mail would come there first. We did not enter port. The Skipper did wire and ask our mail be sent ahead to Bizerte. Seems our ship always left one day before the big enemy plane raids or came into port the day after a big raid. This happened on the way to Dellys and now coming back by Oran, Algiers and at Bizerte. In all places, we missed the biggest raids. The day after the transports pulled out of Oran, the bombers came. Could have been they knew the prisoners had left port. They did know our every move. Radio reports from Berlin and Axis Sally were fairly accurate. Our ships had numbers, no names, yet Sally would give the number and its name while you were looking at them in Oran and her in Berlin.

After two months of going up and down the coast of North Africa, one could see the might in ships being greatly increased. More warships, more transports, cargo vessels, and tankers. Even a hospital ship made its appearance. The cleanup, the cleanout, and the buildup were readily observed. As we passed and could see the city of Algeria, an ammunition ship was still burning from a recent air raid or something. She was being towed to deeper water and out of the harbor. She did blow sky high this late afternoon. The blast was terrific. Later, we found via radio news, she was British and sabotage was the cause of fire. Sometimes in a port, a ship anchored outside break waters would go up in a roar and ball of fire. Divers would dive and tie charges to the ship's screw and any movement would result in an explosion.

After arriving in Bizerte, the mail was waiting. Only there was so much unloaded, we waited for it to be sorted for two days. Suddenly orders came to go to sea for minesweeping for three days. Finally, on June 17, 1943, we came into port. The next day, volunteers went ashore to help secure the mail. 34 letters and packages were received. The one big mental strain had eased. Some letters came there after 2-3 days from the States. Others took a month via boat.

Many ships of numerous nations and countries were collecting in this area, and we knew the same thing was happening in every other port. No big air raids, but little ones three or four times per week. Rumors of other landings and invasions were fast and furious. First it was the Southern Coast of France. Then Sicily and then Italy. Everyone agreed these many ships weren't on a pleasure cruise or a homecoming get together. This ship of ours pretty well defined its own destiny. The largest minesweeper afloat. Sea going to anywhere. Could go into and through only 8 feet of water. Best sweeping gear afloat. A leader for clearing for any attempted landing. Only left to guess where it would be.

We knew after or just before the fall of North Africa, many German "Flying" box car planes were shot down after leaving Cape Bon and Bizerte. Each loaded with 100 soldiers. They were called "The Duck Shoot." Just like sitting ducks on a pond. Being so very slow but powerful. Some were towing gliders loaded with men. It was said some 30-40 were destroyed over the sea and on the ground.

About June 20, 1943, a second trip was made inland to Mateur. A very noticeable change had taken place over the area previously traveled. The city of Mateur was simply alive with activities. Many buildings had been repaired. Business shops set up, streets cleared of rubble and mines. Bridges were rebuilt and the war booty and waste had been cleared from the countryside. A narrow-gauge railroad was in operation. New engines and rolling freight cars of all kinds were in operation. These sergeants who became operating engineers on this railroad were having a picnic. Seems the whistle cord became stuck in their hands. Very familiar tunes were tried with the whistle while rolling along at top speed—say 30-35 miles per hour. As mentioned before, these trains were shipped from state side. Our army engineers wasted no time in repairing, building, etc.

After loading our requisitioned army truck with supplies, we went one mile south of Mateur to the war booty dump and collecting grounds for war material. Must have covered 15-20 acres of ground. Guards were stationed around the fence and at the gates. All enemy helmets were stacked in a big pile 15-20 feet high. Rifles, all the stocks broken, in another pile, field guns in another stack. Larger field pieces - artillery, tanks, trucks, etc., were neatly lined up in row after row. Some guns, etc. were still crated in packing grease. Most had been made unusable by the enemy just before capture. This was where the first German jeep was seen. It had very large balloon tires for traveling on sand. In raising the hood, we first found a motor not there but in the rear. In the area visited, the guard turned for a few minutes while we selected a few souvenirs. Mine were 13 Mauser rifles that were still in the factory packing grease and a new helmet.

A funny thing happened at the supply depot. It was a very big place. Only one metal building for certain supplies. Most all the shoes were in one end of the building. Pairs and sizes were tied with their strings. We were to get a pair for each man aboard ship. These "Brogans" or field shoes and boots were a couple sizes larger than ones of regular size. A hazardous guess is that there were two or three box cars full of shoes in one end of this building. A very small portion of the total supplies at this base was in this building. Rows upon rows, with aisles for trucks to drive through, covered the hillside. All boxes were weather proof of a tar like paper. We discovered the boxes or row of "hard candy". We'd just drive by and select things and into the truck it would go. Ted Oie (storekeeper) got a couple boxes of this candy and started for a third when from nowhere a sergeant stepped out and said that will do. This candy was divided among the ship's crew.

The park or city square of Mateur was covered with a lot of very, very old olive trees. Trenches were all through this grove. In one trench were three shiny 88mm German shells. They looked so pretty and new. What a souvenir these three would make. No, they were booby trapped or someone would have gotten them before. There were two new Mark IV German Tiger tanks on flat cars at the depot. They were burned out inside. One tank had one bullet hole about the size of a middle finger. A hand-cranked machine gun was dismantled and taken with me. After getting back aboard ship, the gunner cleaned and put it into operating condition. It was about our 22-caliber size. They used it to shoot close to the side of tanks where anyone would try to get on the tank. Each turn of the crank it would fire four times.

Very late that afternoon, we returned to our ship at Bizerte. The Skipper had me draw names among the crew members for 12 of my 13 German Mauser rifles. Left me with one. Said we had advantage in getting to go on these trips and one must divide. What a fright to see a Navy crew wearing Army garb of Khaki - some too small, some too large, and all the swapping.

One and only one chance presented itself for Protestant church service this Sunday afternoon at 1600 (4 pm). If other services were ever available, we did not know it. The Skipper and several boys went to early Mass for Roman Catholics. We only tied up at dock side when taking on oil, supplies, etc. Otherwise, we anchored in midstream. This beautiful Sunday afternoon, some 12-14 of us Protestant boys went ashore in the ship's "whale" boat. We walked into the city through and over rubble and around roped off areas to an unbelievable looking building. Only part of a roof still hanging, two walls standing. Some boarding was done on the knocked down sides. The sun shined down on us. Whether it was originally a church, one couldn't tell. The chaplain was about 25 years old. Other boys from other ships were there. He had a few song books along with a black box-like suitcase. A little altar with an empty cross was unfolded. No music to sing with but believe me, those boys did a lot of good singing. The chaplain was a regular "song bird". Maybe it meant we were all "hungry". You know, "where two or more are gathered together." This place, time and gathering would cause any unbeliever to believe. After a good sermon, we trudged and picked our way back to the ship.

For several weeks, our ship was very inactive. That is, we stayed in port more. You see we had "received" and many more ships were arriving almost daily. Lots of help and still more coming. Lake Ferryville was almost full of ships. In the channel and outside the harbor were many large ships. Even British cruisers, corvettes, cargo vessels, etc.

Most all harbors from here to Oran were full of ships. All merchant or cargo vessels of the British carried "Barrage Balloons". Looked funny to us. These were high up over the ship and the balloon had many long steel wires hanging. This was to entangle planes flying low. Their ships' stacks always smoked. We never liked this, because a submarine could see us for miles over a horizon. They were okay though.

July 4, 1943

Spent aboard ship in mid-channel, Bizerte, Tunisia. Such a beautiful day. All of us recalled previous Independence Days on a glorious Fourth of July at our hometowns and states. What a "mixture" one found aboard any ship. This one was no exception. Different nationalities, personalities, tastes, looks, likes, and dislikes, but politically the same. Before leaving the States we received aboard 12 new men to replace crew members for various reasons. All these men's surnames began with the letter 'z'. Homesickness could be cut with a knife. This inactivity hurt morale where men are all so close together. This was not to last long - one had only to look out to the "cloud on the horizon."

July 5, 1943

Only one day late for "celebration" of a Fourth of July. Everyone knew the Axis were up to date on our every plan and move. As previously mentioned, Axis Sally in her broadcast told all. Just as if she were sitting with us and giving the description. All other theaters of war, she gave information about. She would never say where this mighty armada of ships was going to leave for very soon. Just said "we" are ready and before it is too late, you boys had better go back home. Over 340 ships were in our vicinity of all sizes and types. Lately, a Photo Joe had been flying over us taking pictures almost from sunrise to sunset.

Then the fighters and bombers came. Many times, just a few planes made raids at different times. This just disgruntled us. But this night, about 9 p.m., they just kept coming and coming. Most of the ports in North Africa where the invasion fleet had built up, experienced big raids. First the army searchlights came on and probed the sky. A light in an artillery battery would be on for only a short time and then go off because of the risk of becoming a target for an enemy fighter.

There were many a battery of these lights even far inland. First, the largest caliber guns fired before any others. Meant the planes were high and far off. Then the next largest, and then the smaller. Several Messerschmitt fighter planes came in low and hung their "lanterns". These flares, on parachutes, lighted the night as if it were noon day. We tried to shoot these down. They were just dropping more and more. They were crisscrossing these flares, like hanging them on a clothes line. One could read normal print on top deck, it was so bright. One had the feeling to stay in the shadows. These large search lights would converge on the bombers, and when one had probed and made the finding, the planes would try to evade them. The first plane seen hit was just like pictures at the movies—first a "puff" of white smoke, then black smoke and then a string of fire. They would wobble, looking like a falling leaf, and then come straight down to earth. Never once was a parachute sighted. Usually these hits brought a yell from the gun crews and a lot of black slapping.

Our night fighters would go up and head for sea toward the enemy's bases. After the bombers left for home, they would be challenged. This night, in our area, 36 planes bombed us. Guns shot down 5 and the fighters got 12 more known. The first bomb known to hit, hit a big pile of lumber that was being unloaded onto the dock. It burned furiously. Several ships were burning here and there. One can recall the many metal fragments on our ship's deck. It had to be swept off. It hit our helmets like a thrown rock. If one can imagine these 300 to 400 ships' guns firing at one time and the fewest guns any ship had was three, then it can be better envisioned of the noise and display in the heavens. It was estimated over 2160 guns on ships were firing for these some 45 minutes. Fast as they could be loaded.

This night was a nightmare to many a sailor. About midnight and again just before sunup these boys came to visit us again. The raids were from fewer planes and of a shorter duration. The enemy knew a big convoy was heading for new landing on one of the shores they occupied. This we were detailed on the mid-afternoon of July 5, 1943.

Invasion of Sicily

The skipper had spent most of every previous day ashore for a detailed briefing on our part we were to play in an invasion. The ship's company was mustered on the fan tail for the captain's long awaited details. Very briefly we were detailed on what was to happen on the morning of July 6, 1943. My medical records and all other permanent files of other divisions were to be taken ashore for safekeeping and survival if the ship was lost. This was done as directed. There were to be three landings on the south and east coast of Sicily. The Americans would be between areas of the British and Canadians.

Our beach was at Licata, Sicily. It was only 180 miles away. Our ship, the Sentinel, was to lead into the beach and sweep the mine fields for the invasion boats to follow. Two of our sister ships were to follow us to take our place if we didn't make it. This sounded hazardous and it was. Our work, our daily lives had been just that for months. We wanted to get back home and there was a long row to hoe yet. Our one great hope was to go in at high tide. This would let our ship pass over the mine field and cut them loose, then they would bobble to the top and could be seen and destroyed, or dodged.

This great armada of ships began streaming out into the sea at sunup. Some 3200 ships total. The largest invasion force under way at one time during War II. Ships appeared from all those ports down the coast to the west and "The Rock". Even fresh convoys from the States and England were timed to be in this area at this time and date. The convoy of ships covered an area of some 15 square miles.

Activity for men in war is very vital. All were busy about their duties and anxious to have it over with. On a trip like this, we proceeded in complete radio silence. All ships were provided with "walkie-talkie" radios. All galley fires were out. Never any smoking on top side at night.

Our three cooks prepared small mountains of sandwiches, and coffee was plentiful. This was delivered to the men at battle stations. Canned fruit was plentiful but nothing hot for these 4-5 days ahead. For weeks, the Doc could see himself and his men becoming thin and boney. At all battle stations and gun nests, first aid kits were placed. Men from the divisions as electricians, cooks, engineers, deck force, etc. were given lessons in first aid. You see there are two ideas principally in war. Try to destroy the other man and yet survive yourself.

This July 6, 1943, started out just as any other weather wise. During the day, ships were in several directions as far as the eye could see and further. It all looked like one big confusion. They were finding their places in the convoy or armada. Then the most severe storm on the Mediterranean Sea in over 25 years set in. I can only recall that all at once, the storm was there like falling from heaven. We only had to travel 180 miles. We were due to strike on the morning of the 8th.

The ships were scattered. The smaller ships suffered most. The "LCT" (Landing Craft Tanks) with one or two Sherman tanks aboard, would fill and sink like a rock. Many ships were damaged and helpless, bobbing like a cork in the water. The waves were 12-16 feet high. The trough or valley between them was so deep over our ship, when down in one of them, one couldn't see the other ships when standing on top side. It was 16 feet from the top side of our ship to the water. The "LCI" (Landing Craft Infantry) ships really suffered and the soldiers aboard were all sea sick. These ships had flat bottoms. Just before running onto the beach in a landing, the anchor would be dropped from the stern and after unloading it could pull itself off the beach and back into the water. Each carried 110 invasion soldiers with a Navy crew.

Finally, after milling around and around off the coast of Sicily for four days and waiting abatement of the storm, we headed in. Our ship U.S.S. Sentinel #113 led the way. In the darkness, the outline and (if recalled correctly) Mount Etna was visible in the East. After steaming at full speed, toward the beaches and then turning port (left), we went near land that had very high and steep cliffs. Just then three very large Italian search lights came on and lighted up the sea and ships as if day. The feeling was indescribable. A sickness never experienced before came over every body. It was known these lights were there. The air force was supposed to have knocked them out, but the weather prevented it. Also, the large coastal batteries were there and we knew it. After so many feet, yards, or miles of going along the coast, we turned port again and headed out to sea.

Why their guns never fired a single shot was never known. These lights were of the War I carbon type. One could see them burn their carbon stick down and then be replaced. Our ships never fired at them. For what seemed to be an eternity, they all went off and never came on again. The boys were landing. Ships were going in the trail we had made and parking on the beach like a line of autos parking on a football parking lot. In the meantime, C47 planes pulling gliders loaded with men came in over and to the south of the invasion fleet. They were supposed to have already been there. The weather delayed them and had blown them off their course. So what? Our ships thought them to be the enemy and began blasting them out of the sky. Some one hundred met this fate. War is confusion and when not timed just right it becomes more so. One can't help but recall a similar invasion in June 1944 when the weather and confusion prevailed. It all was simply an attempt to overpower the foe.

What great relief we had in having done our job so successfully, and now we had been ordered, as planned, to proceed to a position back behind the invasion armada to do anti-submarine patrol to protect the rear of the invasion force. Our ship was also one of the better armed ships afloat for sub destroying. We carried 600-pound TNT cans (called ash cans) that could be dropped, over the stern, going at full speed (14 knots), on a sub and destroy it. On the end of a "can" was a dial that could be set to go off at any given depth. They were in racks at the stern and were tripped and permitted to roll off one at a time from the bridge (captain). They could be tripped and permitted to roll off at the stern if an electrical failure appeared. Even at full speed and one to 300 yards from their explosion, it would cause our ship to jump out of the water. One had to walk or stand on tip toes to take the jar out of it. It was known ankles were fractured if this was not done.

No submarine was ever sighted by any of our crew in this area. The rough weather prevented the subs from operating or firing torpedoes. They must now be near the surface, and any torpedo jumping waves gets off course. As the hours passed by and we watched the fireworks from some 20 miles at sea, the east began to lighten up. The storm subsided and the sea became pleasant swells. The progress of our boys could be seen as they progressed inland from the sea. The large guns were giving it to them. Firing some 10 to 15 miles ahead of our boys. The projectile could be followed far into the distance like a falling planet.

"The Rains"—The Sentinel Sinks

After day break, it was found the "Maddox", a destroyer, was near us. She was ahead patrolling, as we were, doing the usual zigging and zagging. All others were far off, some 5-8 miles. These placid and quiet moments were short lived. Sometime near 6 a.m., the Maddox, a very new destroyer of the latest design, suddenly began firing her guns. Then, like a flash, she went sky high from a terrific explosion. A German 109 Messerschmitt had dropped a bomb down her stack and the thing made her go up in a ball of fire and smoke. 312 men were aboard her. When we passed over her watery grave, not a sign of a man was to be seen. It could have been no more than three minutes that passed until we were there as we were sort of following her. They never knew what hit her. (1964 the Gulf of Tonkin, Vietnam incident involved a new USS Maddox which destroyed North Vietnam torpedo boats). The hunting in these parts, where there were such few ships, for the Nazi was good. These 109 fighters had "anti-personnel" bombs meant for the landing troops on the beaches. It was "too hot" there, so they came out behind the invasion force. They carried 20 mm guns also.

After finishing off the Maddox, two Italian War I type sea planes were sighted coming at us flying just above the water. We fired at them with our 3-inch guns and they turned away and were never seen again. Then came "the Rains". Three German 109s came at us. All our guns from the side of their attack were firing at them. They would dive, strafing our decks and then drop their bombs when pulling out of the dive. The first bomb or stick of three, found its mark. This first of three bombs hit in front of the bow, the next hit amidships and the third hit a few feet off the stern and to the port (left) of our ship. The first bomb sprayed water on us, the second did not explode but lodged between two diesel motors, and the third exploded so near the ship, a 6 by 8-foot hole was blown in the Sentinel's side at the stern. Our rudder was jammed and out of control. We were still going full speed and while zigging and zagging, we were at the time zagging or turning to the port (left). So, this jammed rudder made us go in circles to the left. Having two engine rooms of two motors each, one room forward and one aft meant now only half speed. The aft engine room became flooded and was sealed off. That is the water tight doors were closed and locked forever. She began to "list" to the port and stern (rear) almost immediately as this room filled with water.

The first casualty known to me was the Engineering Officer. A Mr. Marz or Martz. He was from Detroit, Michigan, and in peacetime a tug boat captain on the Detroit River. We were very close shipmates. So very vividly can it be recalled when he was first seen. All casualties were to be brought to the Doc in the mess hall, the main battle dressing station and all major dressings, etc. But this man was different. He was sort of crawling and pulling himself in my direction. He was grinning or trying to smile as one had always seen him the first time on any given day. He said "Doc, I have been hit. Do you have a cold glass of beer?" Undoubtedly, a 20-mm shell had hit him and exploded in his midsection. Morphine was given and a large battle dressing applied front and back. Life gradually drained away. He asked how bad it was. He was told very bad. He still was witty and asked for "a cold glass of beer."

Very soon it was learned there were many casualties. The 109s were still coming at us, doing a figure 8 each trip. Being below deck, one could always tell their coming. The guns would quiet and away they would go again. This one shell or bomb that failed to explode and lodged between the motors in the forward engine room, caused a really good scare to the board control room and platform engineer. His name was Simmons. This control panel was just above the engines and his back was to them. Instead of answering the bells or signals from the skipper on the bridge, he was up one deck with me, telling me of that "thing" on the engine that was at his back and just down below him. He was very excited and who wasn't. The engine room and bomb were directly below where we were standing.

Finally, he was convinced it wasn't going to explode and for him to return before the Captain got angry. This boy Simmons was to become a papa for the first time this very date July 10, 1943. He had talked about it all the time if anyone would listen. He never lived to see or know whether he was blessed with that son. Very shortly after his leaving, he came back to me crying and rocking up and down on the mess table. Saying "I can't breathe." He crumpled at my feet. It was thought later that Simmons died of a heart attack. No visible signs showed.

By this time the ship was listing badly to port. The deck below my station was burning. The 109 shells were setting our bed clothing on fire in our quarters just forward of me and below. The heat had begun to blister and buckle on our mess hall floor. The "hot foot" was getting hotter. The wounded and dead were everywhere around and outside the mess hall door. The ship had listed so far now that the swells in the sea were breaking over the ship railing and coming through the opened door. One man lay across the door sill. All wounded or dead were brought down and left nearby. The able bodied must return to their guns. The Bureau of Medicine and Surgery used the slogan "Keep as many men at as many guns as many days as possible." Some were patched up and sent back up. Others deemed unfit were laid aside or sat at the mess table benches. Had one wounded boy from Birmingham, Alabama that was really more scared than in pain.

Morphine in small tubes was plentiful. Each contained a one gram dose. All stations over the ship had them. The "students" or one who had been given lessons would give any injured man a shot. But this Alabama boy came in screaming his eyes were out, he could not see. His scalp from back to front was peeled from his skull and was hanging over his eyes. Hence he could not see. This was taken care of and he could see once more, and all was well. For he was sitting on the table next to the bulk head (wall) when a 109 came by and knocked him off again.

The fighter would sort of side slip when firing and across the deck where most of us were. These holes in the bulk head were about finger size and three feet apart. The noise of these bullets going around and around inside this compartment was incredible. For as one could tell, many were spared in between these spaces where the bullet came through.

One terrific and very different noise stands out plainly. A bomb hit on the galley. The noise all those pans and dishes made! This one boy, our ship fitter second class, had been patched up and put out of action. He was placed next to and leaning back against the "scuttle butt" (drinking fountain). Delfario was born in Naples, Italy and hoped to visit there one day. He never made it. This bomb that hit in or near the galley got him. While dressing one man's broken arm, splinting it, we were standing near a 6-inch pipe support. A shell had exploded and it ended it all for him. This post afforded a deflection area for me. Only shrapnel in my back and sitting place.

The deceased were piled in one corner to the side where the ship was listing. At last count seven were there. In all we had eleven dead and 54 wounded for a total of 65 out of 99 men aboard. Two of every three were dead or injured. Of the injured, 16 were stretcher cases.

One of the most unbelievable realities became known. Water being everywhere and not a drop to drink. Well, nearly not a drop to drink. The day before we departed for this invasion, all water flasks were drained and aired. At this very moment, all were still "airing," for we had failed to fill them. These water flasks were literally all over the ship—empty. In the motor boat, life rafts, gun stations, etc. all flasks were still airing. One must try to imagine the great need for water especially among the wounded. Even the excitement would cause craving for water. The only water found aboard was the ice trays in the Officers' box and the one in the cook's shack. This water was rationed a spoonful at a time only to those wounded, and the most serious ones first. "Mouth cotton" was a dime a bale.

After some 40-50 minutes of beating, we were left helpless and burning at sea by the 109s. This was my first trip outside my station. The attack started about 6 a.m. and this must have been near 10 a.m., when those inside were cared for as best as one could. The men in our gun's nest, above the main deck and on what looked like wings as protruding platforms, were wounded with some dead. The ship's yeoman named Batson (Dallas, TX) told me to check Oie our ship's storekeeper who was a gunner right above us. Oie (Ted) was six foot, six inches tall, the maximum height taken into the Navy. This 20-mm gun he operated had shields on either side of the gun barrel about 12 inches wide and 18 inches high. This had afforded protection for the lower waist up. But from the waist down his legs were like jelly. His case was hopeless. But he was in no pain. Laid there and talked and joked to the end. In the meantime, he was moved via stretcher to the main deck. The loader for Oie's gun (clip loaded) was a boy named Potaski. Strange as it may seem, this boy was to become a papa this very day July 10, 1943, the same date this boy Simmons was to be papa. He too never knew whether he had been blessed with a child that day. Potaski was the shortest man aboard—five feet tall. We called this gun crew "Mutt and Jeff." The steel gun shield around the gun position was circular. All that was left of this little man (and he was tough) was piled up and covered with his "Mae West" (life jacket).

All the other boys were so very haggard looking. Their eyes and faces looked like a coal miner's. All were willing to help and at the same time they were a silent lot. Maybe dazed and with foggy minds would be better. Then the fatigue must enter somewhere. The ship's bridge was hit hard, being the "bull's eye" of this kind of target. Too, the very heart of a ship is here. The Signalman and all that can be recalled, his name was "Pop" Weekes. He was in War I therefore being in his late 40s. He received a direct hit. He was near the box or storage for the flags. An American flag was nearby and after putting him on a stretcher to bring him down, this boy Batson (Tommy) covered him with this flag. The four metal stretchers and several Army type folding stretchers were all full. We used bunk mattresses and lashed the wounded men to them. The entrance to the crew's quarters was tried for more mattresses, but the fire was too great. All the mattresses from the Officers' quarters were used. The ship was listing very badly.

PHOTOS OF U.S.S SENTINEL SINKING (GOVERNMENT PHOTOS)

The Captain used our "walkie-talkie" radio for the SOS. An "LCI" answered and finally came into view. After circling us, the skipper of this LCI refused to come alongside. He was loaded with soldiers going into Sicily. He said it was too dangerous to stop and be a "sitting duck" for a submarine. On he went. Then an "SC" (sub chaser) appeared and another cheer went up. This little ship was wooden hull and carried 12-14 men. Say 60 foot long and lightly armored. She carried 20 mm guns and 250-pound depth charges (TNT). More danger to subs than they were to her. She sat high and shallow in the water. This little blonde skipper came right alongside on the starboard and we threw him a line. By now, our ship's top deck on the port side was underwater. This used to be 16-20 feet to the water from the railing. She was listing so badly one could hardly walk on the slanted deck. The wounded were quickly lowered over the side onto and into this ship "from heaven". The crew gave up their bunks for the wounded. Some wounded were left on top side and covered with tarps to keep off the sea spray and hot sun.

At 11 a.m. July 10, 1943, the USS Sentinel AM 113 slipped from sight, stern first, and very slowly into a 2300-foot grave. The men aboard her jumped and swam to another SC and were plucked from the sea. They beat us back to Bizerte by one day. We had to travel slower to protect the wounded. The little blonde skipper of this wonderful ship was a Prince.

Before going farther, one young boy (16), last name Paul, left the Sentinel in a very unusual way. When the first attack came, he did a swan dive overboard and just kept going. While our ship was going in circles and we went past him, he would wave while bobbing in the water. He thought we were searching for him. After the Sentinel went dead in the water, we were at the farthest point from him. He was reported overboard in the final report to Washington, D.C. Upon our return to port at Bizerte, all hospitals and incoming ships were checked for him, but we never found him.

On the morning of July 13, 1943, we arrived at the place where one week prior we had departed. The blonde skipper (a lieutenant junior grade) wired of our coming and to have necessary help dockside. About 9 a.m. we docked. Some 7-8 ambulances (Army) were lined up waiting. A 2 or 3 striper came aboard and said now "we take charge." He was told over my dead body. The skipper backed me up. They were briefed about these men and their little-known conditions, and that their condition was known only to me. Things settled down then and the very seriously wounded ones were removed first and so on down the line until all departed for the Army field hospital nearby. Only one boy died of his chest wounds seven days later. His name was Long.

The little blonde skipper and I had a very personal goodbye, and he was never seen by me again. Gone, yet to this day, days past, and for sure days to come, this man surely survived the War and is living somewhere a very healthy and happy man and too recalling the past.

Waiting to Go Home

Every piece of mail, package, letter, or parcel was censored and so stamped before going out. All zones where the enemy operated were censored. This slowed mail. Some letters were book length. For several days, my letters only contained "ok" and signed. We knew a lot of times, the lost ships were reported before next of kin had received those notices that all dreaded. Surely, this did happen to me. The ships Maddox and Sentinel were reported and printed before my mail arrived.

Our ship's (or ex-ship's) company was kept together and housed in a bombed-out building at the airport, near the grounds west of Bizerte where the French Naval Academy was located. When the hospital would discharge a man for further duty, he returned to us. Some were sent home for further treatment or discharge. The survivors of the Sentinel were in on two "firsts". First to return from initial invasion of Sicily to Bizerte and the first to return to the United States from the Sicily invasion.

Again, we were issued Army clothes. All we had was on our person. Even to this day, my helmet, gas mask, and Mae West are stored away safely. We ate here and there at Army field kitchens, Sea Bees kitchens, and K-rations. No duties, like a stray animal wondering and waiting, trying to get someone, any ship, to take us home. Many hours were spent at the airport and docks watching the traffic. Too, it was amusing to sit and listen to the "Axis Sally" broadcast from Berlin of just what was taking place. The ships' numbers there at the docks that were loading were broadcast to us and we were sitting there looking at them.

There was a steady stream of men and material that were being loaded. Bases here were being cleared out and moved nearer the fighting. It was fantastic. The testing range for guns of all makes and kinds that were captured, was near our "house". We watched them a lot. Here is where the German small caliber shells made of wood were seen. This bullet would explode on contact and the splinters in one's body would become very infectious after a few days—usually fatal. The Germans denied having or ever using these. Two or three sizes were held in my hand. For one thing, the German guns were not "inferior" weapons. This goes back to the Mauser rifle retrieved from the Mateur battle fields and other items that were lost when our ship went down. No other souvenirs were ever attempted again even though there were plenty and some boys even selling them.

Daily, rumors were passed and our group would go aboard one of the many ships coming and going. Finally, the old War I ship we captured from the Germans and renamed it the "Chateau Thierry" loaded us aboard. This was about August 11, 1943. She headed west toward Oran. After arriving there, we were unloaded and put aboard the USS Merak. The Chateau Thierry was loaded with German prisoners for delivery to the States. Of all things, the Merak, a passenger and refrigeration ship, headed back east to Bizerte.

It is necessary at this time to go back almost one year to the revelation of an injury to our ship's cook aboard the Sentinel. We were in dry dock in Montreal, Canada, when he fell off the gang plank and broke a leg. He was left in Montreal under the care and direction of the U.S. Embassy. As we were boarding the Merak on one gang plank, here came "Ol' Frenchie" Guthereau down the other gang plank. He had come from the States for further transfer to the Sentinel. It was a big laugh when told he would have to dive 2000 feet to her. He had not heard. He continued on to a receiving station and we went on our way!

Our hearts sank when the Merak headed for Bizerte, the one place we never cared to see again. We were there one day, unloading fresh fruits and meats for the boys. Then back to Oran. The War had very much stopped in these areas now. On to the "Rock", through the straits and into the Atlantic and most certainly in the direction of the States. This was the fastest of convoys, as all ships were very large passenger vessels. There were twelve of us and five destroyers leading the way as escorts. Felt good to be escorted instead of escorting, and going west toward home.

These liners carried German prisoners of war. One day one of the ships buried 4-5 at sea. All hands on all ships (not on duty) would report to top deck and stand at attention, while taps was played, and the prisoners were slid into the sea from the stern. Several times the prisoners rioted, even committed suicide. They were afraid down below decks a sub would sink the ship. All of them believed Adolph that the sea had been cleared of Allied ships and any that showed itself would go down. Some of the prisoners couldn't believe what they saw: so very many ships and looking spick and span.

Oh, the food aboard this ship, USS Merak, was so very good. Long-needed rest was to be had and absorbed. A bunk to sleep in again. A canteen to buy "Pogie-bait" (candy) and cigars. They had ice cream aboard -made it themselves. The first day aboard all its production was for the enjoyment of their "guests." About the second day aboard, good fortune came my way. Kept noticing while in the "chow" line a familiar face. Found out it was a boy who worked in the machine shop at Ford Motor in Dallas. A nice reunion was had and he took me under his wing, and the best was offered and had. A long-remembered thing happened one night. This boy and two or three others had a great feast. We went to the "bilges," the very bottom of the ship near the drive shaft of the ship's screw. They had a large round crate of cheese, a ham, and crackers. What a feast and one that continued later. All at once the ship rattled and bounced, making all kinds of unfamiliar noises. Talk about coming up an escape hatch 4 or 5 decks quickly!

The ship wasn't hit as we had feared. The five destroyers were dropping depth charges nearby. Sometimes subs would get under ships to avoid detection. Those "wolf packs" (group of subs) would try to attract the escorts with one sub while the others would go in for the kill. Those "scavengers" of the seas (destroyers) always did a good job and this crossing was no exception. 26 days it took to go over and only nine to return.

Arrived in New York on August 20, 1943. Even received pay aboard Merak. We had retrieved all our records left in Bizerte before the invasion of Sicily. New York and the "Ol' Lady" still holding the torch. The tears literally flowed from many eyes and none tried to hide them. This must have been, before and after, repeated on many ships many times.

Puerto Rico

We disembarked at Pier #92. This pier was next to the French liner "Normandie" that had sunk while we were refitting her for war service. She was taken while in port when the war started. She lay on her side and stayed there during the War. The third largest liner afloat before the War. We were immediately issued a complete outfitting of clothing while at Pier 92. Many welcomed liberties in New York. Then a 30-day leave of absence and home. It was called "Survivor's Leave."

After this leave of absence, I returned to Pier 92 for further duty. On October 6, 1943, orders for Roosevelt Roads Naval Station, Ensenada Honda, Puerto Rico were received. This was duty at the Naval Dispensary on this eastern end of the island. The war had long before left this area. Boarded the USS Yukon for this trip. The Yukon was a passenger and fruit vessel plying between the States and South America during peacetime. Now the Navy had requisitioned her for war duty. Every two weeks, she made a trip south from New York. One destroyer always escorted her. Arrived in Bermuda on October 10th, departed on the 14th, arrived in Port Au Prince, Haiti on the 15th and departed the same day for Puerto Rico. This was a mail, supply, and passenger ship on a bi-monthly trip. Arrived in San Juan, Puerto Rico on October 17, 1943. Also, departed for Roosevelt Roads on the 17th and arrived at the other end (east) of the island the same day.

This end of the island was a secret base. A dry dock had been constructed here to take the British ships "Queen Mary" and "Queen Elizabeth" if never needed for repair. These two ships were used during the war to ferry our boys over to England and return the wounded. They traveled along, never with escort. They were so very fast, submarines couldn't catch them. To my knowledge, these ships never used the dock. They carried about 12,000 men and made fast, quick trips from England about every 10-11 days. So even if the dock was never used, the insurance in having facilities if needed was well worth it.

This base was principally a "Sea-Bee" base. This Navy group was construction men trained to defend themselves. Many times, it was said, these construction men would be or were ashore to greet most of our landings around the world. This dispensary was mostly a first aid station with a small operating room and ward with 6-8 beds.

The duty here was good. Yes, and so very quiet and restful. Here my promotion to Chief Pharmacist's Mate was made. The best rate in the Navy. Top kick of the enlisted men. Top pay, more privileges, private quarters, better food. This base only called for one chief, so orders came once more for me. So on December 12, 1943, I reported to the Naval Hospital in San Juan, Puerto Rico for duty.

This was "uptown" on the other end of the island to the west. This 100-bed hospital had just been completed and was being furnished.

The reason for being in "quiet" places for duty was because while at Pier 92, a directive from Washington gave men who were survivors from war zones a choice for duty in "quiet waters." All this was my choice. My duty at San Juan Naval Hospital oversaw supplies and equipment. The storeroom with seven men was my "baby". Here at the hospital is where the Purple Heart caught up with me. The hospital's commanding officer was supposed to pin it on me at a ceremony before the staff. This was never done. Just put it away until this day.

The weather on this island was so very wonderful. Temperature varied about 6-8 degrees during the year. Most always in the 70s. The war being two years old now, yet there was no rationing of any kind on this island. Silk hose, tires, shoes, etc. were plentiful and all you wanted to buy. Seemed strange when remembered in the States the strict rationing. One day, while at the supply depot downtown, we went to pick up the hospital beds and a boy who once was a former shipmate waited on us. It was Johnnie Johnson. We were shipmates in Norfolk Naval Hospital, Portsmouth, Virginia back in 1933. In fact, we attended President Roosevelt's Inauguration together on March 4, 1933. His first term and the last President to be inaugurated on a March 4th. We had a very pleasant visit just "re-hashing" our time as shipmates and the years since.

Trinidad, British West Indies

This duty here lasted only a short while. On January 17, 1944, I departed for Escort Repair Base Dispensary, Trinidad, British West Indies. Further south and very near South America. This was one of the bases America received or leased for 99 years when England received the War I destroyers in exchange. These bases we built on various islands in the Caribbean Sea were very beneficial to the British. They were hard hit on the British Isles from air raids. Their ships were repaired here just as ours were.

The island was very beautiful. The weather wonderful and pleasant. Again, the average temperature was and stayed around 74 degrees year-round. We were so near the equator, the days and nights varied by only six minutes. All nationalities of the world were in Trinidad. All tropical fruits were plentiful. Pulled and ate bananas from a tree while standing on the barrack's porch. The natives would climb a coconut tree and throw down coconuts for their lunch. Many, many coconut groves were over the island. The United Fruit Company operated most groves.

This island was one of the three crossroads of the world. The bay which the base overlooked was a natural harbor. All the fleets of the world would have room to anchor there at one time. The "Dragon's Mouth" at the entrance toward the coast of South America could be easily well-protected. We were told that in early 1943, one or two subs got through the "mouth" and destroyed five tankers one evening. They or it escaped too. This bay is where the sea planes landed when one arrived from San Juan for duty. The Axis Powers had long ago left these waters and never returned.

The dispensary duty was great. Had two doctors and 12 mates (corpsmen). 12-14 beds comprised our ward capacity. A Dental unit and two dentists. The dentist once told me the equipment for this unit was sent via ship and was sunk on three of four tries. Sick call at nine and then most of the day was free. Only one man on watch to care for emergencies.

The mosquitoes or their breeding places were constantly sprayed. Still, they were thick and the malaria type took their toll. The birds were very plentiful and of all varieties. Something that was not so on the Island of Puerto Rico. Mongoose (small animal) were brought onto the island to rid it of poisonous snakes and after clearing them out, got all the birds. Now they were trying to control the mongoose.

I had a macaw bird here at the escort repair base that another chief left with me. I accepted an offer by a merchant seaman for $500 - couldn't keep him because of restrictions on parrots and parrot fever. "Joe" the parrot could say about anything and did. Had 17 shades and colors. The island had many boa and python snakes. Many of the boys hunted them but for me, never much of a hunter. A local boy, who

57

drove our ambulance, came in one morning crying. Said a python had swallowed one of his brothers. They certainly were known to swallow a 20-pound pig.

This city was British. Downtown was pretty nice. Good buildings and clean parks. The majority of its people lived in huts and on the water's edge. The filth was unbelievable. Average wage was thirty cents per day. We needed workers on our base and the agreement was to use a given number of locals at thirty cents per hour. A Naval Air Station and base hospital was situated on this island. The trade winds blew constantly giving this area one of the ideal climates of the world. The rainy season lasted about three months out of the year.

This June 6, 1944, was a memorable day. A very close watch was being kept on the war's progress in the Mediterranean Sea and elsewhere. Italy proper had been invaded and the slow progress of climbing "the boot" was in progress. This date, while taking a nap under my mosquito netting, the radio program suddenly changed. The coast of France had been invaded by the Allied forces. A great deal of feeling and very deep appreciation was felt for the hordes of ships and men that were then and there landing on the shores of a strange country. The only feeling of relief for these men was two-fold — the long preparation and just waiting had come to an end. Then two, the remaining days when most could return home, were fewer and fewer. This English Channel invasion and then the invasion of the southern coast of France, meant that on many fronts the enemy would be pushed to final victory.

Back to the Atlantic—USS Oswald

This cozy duty and quiet atmosphere came to an end on July 2, 1944. I boarded the USS Antares for Pier 92 again. Back tracked my route when coming here. From Trinidad, to Puerto Rico, to Haiti, Bermuda, and then New York. Arrived in New York on July 11, 1944. On July 12, 1944, I received another 30-day leave, and on August 11, 1944, this leave of absence ended. Orders were waiting me for sea duty again. Left New York on August 15, 1944 and reported to the Boston Naval Yard August 16th for duty aboard the USS Oswald, DE 767.

The name "Oswald" if recalled correctly, was a seaman's name (maybe a Sea Bee) the ship was named for. He was awarded a high medal for bravery. Also, lost his life. Nothing can be found of this Oswald being any relation to Lee Harvey Oswald. The Oswald had a painted, color picture of Oswald the Rabbit and his carrot on the stack. She carried a complement of 312 men. A very fast ship of 18 knots plus.

U.S.S Oswald (Government Photo)

August 18, 1944, we departed for Londonderry, Ireland. This ship had been doing convoy duty to Europe. Even though she had been painted for Pacific Ocean duty, she was repainted and stayed on the East Coast. All hands were glad of this, for we knew the States would be visited often. The convoy we escorted this trip was a fast one. Five escorts and 15-18 tankers and passenger ships. The usual north Atlantic weather was encountered after passing across the Gulf Stream and its many miles of seaweed. The many, many porpoises are always ready and willing to play with any ships.

When nearing the coast of the southern and west coast of England, there was a report that a pack of subs was in our path. At this stage of the war, Germany had recalled her subs from many foreign areas and brought them closer to home or to shipping crossroads. This was one of those points where their subs were thick. Suddenly, our convoy turned and headed west toward the States again. For one day and night, we turned this direction and the other. Finally, we proceeded toward the mouth of the Channel. Part of our convoy went to Plymouth, England, and our portion continued north up the west coast of Ireland.

The Irish were neutral and yet anti-English. They were pro-American and pro-Nazi. Just didn't like England from long standing. Londonderry was on the northern tip of Ireland and down a river inland some 20-30 miles. While we cruised up the beautiful coast of Ireland, a radio tower could be seen on a hill the Nazi were using. The Irish permitted the Nazis to establish bases on their coast. A peculiar feeling to travel close by an enemy radio station and sub nest. Everything went well until this late afternoon when the tankers were entering the anti-submarine nets and mine fields - a sub picked off the very last tanker in the line. She blew sky high. The stern half stayed afloat and our ship remained with it. After ascertaining no one remained aboard, we sunk her. This was at 10 p.m. in the evening. The sun was still shining. Finally, we entered through the nets and mine field, on to Londonderry.

The people were very friendly. Here all the homes join together and are multiple stories. A chimney on each roof top like an old "churn". All were of the same construction material and design. Hedges or rocks were their fences. Everything looked centuries old and most were. This city was once a large Sea Bee base. Since the Channel invasion, their base was empty.

After arriving here August 30, 1944, and a visit of two days, we went to the Irish Sea. Visited Glasgow, Scotland, where other empty ships were picked up for the return trip home (USA). Tankers were filled with water after emptying their oil cargo. This is to balance her and help take the heavy sea. The North Atlantic is always rough and at times very rough waters.

We departed for the States on September 5, 1944. Mostly our convoyed ships were tankers and passenger ships which carried prisoners of war or the wounded. Usually the American wounded were the ones who were being sent home for discharge. While in Scotland and the general area, one could see many fighters and bombers crossing to and from the Channel to Europe. The German Air Force was practically out of effective operation.

No subs were sighted on the return trip. The weather was so bad and a sub can't operate effectively. Several runs were made over objects when the sonar sound gave indications of a large object down deep. The blasting with depth charges gave no indication of any results. A lot of ships had been sunk in many areas and many times the sonar system picked up a "ping" from them. Too, large schools of fish gave the same ping. Most times, our convoy was so fast, we never stayed behind very long to observe the results.

We arrived safely in New York on September 17, 1944. We went immediately to the Brooklyn Naval Shipyards. After a good check and paint job in the yards, we left again for Plymouth, England on October 6, 1944. Again, this was about the same number of ships and escorts in the convoy as the previous one. I must mention here, many ships in the invasion of France back in June were in the Brooklyn Yard for repairs, the battleship Texas being one of them. She had received several hits from shore batteries on her starboard side, and one gaping hole was visible. One 14-inch gun turret looked to be out of commission. She came to the States under her own power.

This trip across to England was uneventful except the very bad weather encountered and a man we lost overboard. For some 8-10 days, no one could go top side, the weather was terrific. On one of these trips, many icebergs were seen. Just before arriving in Plymouth, one day out, one of our seamen was lost overboard. He had his life jacket on one arm and was climbing a ladder on the outside of a gun mount. Using one hand to hold a ladder rung and about the time he reached for a rung, the ship listed away from him suddenly. Left him out in thin air and falling back and away from the ship. He hit the top cable around the ship and this gave him a spring up and out into the ocean. His Mae West fell on top of him in the water. This accident took place forward of bridge on starboard side.

The skipper saw this man fall while going up to his watch station. The skipper disobeyed all the rules of the seas in wartime by simply turning around and going back between the lines of ships to rescue this man. (Man overboard was from Texas—name can't be recalled). Nevertheless, we did just that. In cases of this kind, the procedure was to notify the last ship in the convoy and let them pick up the man. When we left our escort station, this left a gap in the protection screen. All ships in this or like convoys used code names. This trip we were all named for birds. We used the name "Crow." The temperature of the North Atlantic's water permitted a man to live only a few minutes. This boy was a good swimmer and he immediately began swimming fast and in circles to help keep from freezing. When pulling him aboard, under the bottom of three cables, his billfold fell from his hip pocket and his wrist watch was stripped from him. Both fell into the "drink". The usual warm blankets, heat and an ounce of whiskey soon had him up and going again. In fact, he threatened to jump overboard again for the booze.

We arrived October 17, 1944 in Plymouth, England. These few days there were so interesting. This port was one of the main "jumping off" places for the invasion. Many ships were shuttling back and forth across the English Channel to France. Droves of planes were doing the same in the sky. The trip into the city was most saddening. Many blocks of business places and homes were barren. In 1940-41, the Germans all but destroyed this city. Raids were infrequent now and by only a few planes at a time. These destroyed buildings were all carted away and the lots appeared cleaned to build again. The climate here is very mild. Seldom freezes. The Gulf Stream swings in near this coastal city. Beautiful gardens were growing in most all vacant dirt spaces. The "Plymouth Rock" site where the Pilgrims departed for America, was visited. The Naval Station, across the bay from the shipyards, was visited. We played the British boys in a soccer game. What a riot and defeat. Those boys are good or we did poorly in a game seldom played in America.

On October 21, 1944, we departed Plymouth for the USA. Must backtrack and mention an occurrence in September 1944. This also answers for the long stay in the Brooklyn Navy Yard from September

17 to October 6, 1944. Just when we were about 100 miles of the New York Ambrose light ships, a hurricane was encountered. The thing was first reported turning into New Jersey and inland. We kept coming west. Then were ordered to turn back east. This we did but it caught us. Winds were 125 miles per hour. All ships were ordered to pull apart and scatter. Some ships lost power. One lost its rudder. The very large ship "Princess of Australia" lost her power. We took three 76 degree lists. She was built to take just that hit. The ship's damage was terrific. All dishes were broken. Gun shields on one side of the ship (starboard) caved in by the movement. Life rafts torn loose and washed to sea. Most of all, paint came off as if sanded off.

The skipper turned the ship's bow almost directly into the wind while going almost full speed ahead, but we still lost ground backwards. The center of the hurricane was calm. That is the wind velocity. The waves were 30 to 35 feet high. The whole hurricane's force passed over us. When it hit or just before, the sea was calm as a mill pond. It was late in the evening. At midnight, we turned to New York again. The next morning, the nearest ship to us was not in our radar range. Its range was some 30 miles. Finally, New York and hence the longer stay in port than usual. Also, the first report of a hurricane broadcast and description from an airplane while flying in the hurricane's eye was made this day. The winds did a lot of damage to the Coney Island entertainment grounds. One could, on a clear day, see the Ferris wheel, etc. on shore from the sea lane. It was reported by one Nazi sub skipper of watching the fun on Coney Island from out at sea.

About November 3, 1944, we arrived again in New York. Before entering any shipyard, a ship must first unload its ammunition of all kinds. This was done on the coast of New Jersey near Bayonne at the depot, and loaded again before leaving. One of the President's sons was a skipper of a destroyer with us. Elliott was his name. We always unloaded or loaded with his ship. The day after our last trip to the ammo depot, a ship blew up from careless handling of explosives at this depot.

My final round trip to England began about November 6, 1944. We went to Southampton, England. Most days when away from the Gulf Stream the weather was our worst enemy. The subs were about a thing of the past. Either sunk or called in close to home. The "Casablanca" type aircraft carriers were plentiful at this time. They were small carriers. Some converted from another type of ship. Simply a flight deck would be put on top of the ship. Some would just roam around in the ship lanes and the planes would go out sub hunting. Some traveled in convoys. Planes from land bases roamed far at sea. The enemy bomber was about a thing of the past. Keeping up war supplies was easier and they were more plentiful. Navy ships were going to and unloading on the coast of France at Cherbourg, Le Havre, etc.

Arrived in Southampton about November 19, 1944. This beautiful day was spent in Southampton Harbor. The white cliffs of Dover glistened in the sunlight. After delivering our ships, we came back out to Portsmouth, England, only 90 miles from London. Some of our crew were permitted to visit London. My trip was to have been the next day. All was interrupted by a new instrument of war. The "rocket" bomb or "buzz" bomb. These were self-propelled and came from secret bases in France. Late in the afternoon, one of these things hit near the shore and seemed to spray water on us. We immediately pulled anchor and headed for Plymouth. Usually these bombs came in a pattern and covered a large area, so we must have known to move on. The boys who visited London, came to Plymouth and boarded ship. The next day, two or three of us were to visit London, as mentioned. Instead, we sat out the next few days in Plymouth. Really, the waiting for the ships to unload wasn't bad. Liberty to visit ashore was granted and activities in the harbor and in the sky were interesting.

Reports on all fronts were encouraging. The war's later phase was now being entered into. Many ships were being assigned to the Pacific since few, if any, were being lost here. About November 25, 1944, we departed England for America. The usual ships, maybe more passenger vessels, were escorted on our return trip. We arrived back in New York about December 9, 1944. This was my last trip abroad the remainder of the war.

War Ends

Sometime just before Christmas, the "Doc" prepared his transfer papers to "turn in" at the Brooklyn Naval Hospital. For many months, my lumbar back was almost unbearable. The heavy pounding on the ship in this cold, rough weather was about all that could be absorbed. A ruptured disc at the 4th-5th lumbar occurred off Prince Edward Island when our ship listed and threw me between two bunks, face forward. On January 8, 1945, a Dr. Fitsch performed the surgery.

After getting up and around, my assignment was in the hospital storeroom doing paperwork. This gave me liberty every night and weekends off. Saw most of New York. Spring came and New York is pretty this time of year. Saw the Brooklyn Dodgers play baseball for the first time.

About this time, Mr. Roosevelt died (April 13, 1945) and Truman became President. It will always be regretted Mr. Roosevelt did not live to see war's end. I will long remember March 4, 1933, when his inauguration was observed. Then the next day (Sunday), when a boy named Johnson and I stood near his car with Mrs. Roosevelt and his daughter beside him, on their way to church.

While at the hospital, a few days' leave took me again to Washington D.C. for a visit with my sister, Lucille, and her husband, Tommy Guy. Tommy was stationed in a naval school there. About April 15, 1945, the Medical Survey Board called me forward for my "case review". The Admiral Chairman (all were doctors) of the Board wanted to send me home. I protested that the war wasn't over, and my little bit of help might still be needed. I was determined to stay until the war's end. Too, it was known that those with a disability could serve in a limited capacity.

The Board granted my wish and limited duty was permitted. Too, a limited duty man could select any station or ship nearest his place of enlistment. About April 22, 1945, orders were issued to report to a receiving ship in New Orleans, Louisiana for further transfer to the Public Service Hospital, Fort Worth, Texas. Spent one day and night in Algiers across the river from New Orleans (8th Naval District). This was the receiving ship where several thousand sailors were "lost". Their papers were lost or misplaced for many months. This was one of the many strange happenings of the war. (While writing this journal, LBJ inaugurated President of the USA on January 20, 1965. Sir Winston Churchill died. Buried the 30th.)

About May 1, 1945, I reported to U.S. Public Service Hospital, Fort Worth, Texas for duty. The Navy had made use of this hospital for treatment of its boys who were mentally ill. Being one of the staff, our duty was to oversee a trainload going to various sections of the U.S. to hospitals near their homes.

My first trip called for me to go to Oregon on May 13, 1945. This trip was never made. The fighting ended in Europe on May 8, 1945. Unconditional surrender and "VE Day" officially declared by all Allies. This day, May 8, 1945, Sir Winston Churchill went before Parliament and offered a resolution thanking "the Almighty" for victory. He disclaimed any victory as being his. The praise being his "maker".

Immediately, all branches of all services issued an order for all "limited duty" personnel to be discharged at once. So, without any further choice and the day before a two-week trip that was to be made to Oregon, my discharge was signed on May 12, 1945.

At this time, a large segment of the war had ended. There seemed a long way to go yet. Still, one could see the full fury of the Allies could be concentrated in one theater to war—the Pacific. This was done when many ships and men were transferred to and toward the country of the "Rising Sun." What seemed to be many remaining days and months were cut rather short. After a test of the first "atomic bomb" near Alamogordo, New Mexico on July 16, 1945, the beginning of the end of the war in the Pacific was near. On August 6, 1945, the second bomb exploded over Hiroshima, Japan. Of 343,000 people, 150,000 dead and injured resulted. This was a U-235 bomb. Three days later, a plutonium 239 bomb was dropped over Nagasaki, Japan. A city of 200,000 people, 79,000 were killed and injured. On August 14, 1945, 7 p.m., marked "V-J Day" and the end of World War II. President Truman announced the unconditional surrender of Japan. September 2, 1945, has since been officially declared V-J Day. For on this date, the Japanese signed the terms of surrender aboard the USS Missouri in Tokyo Bay.

So, the end of the beginning came after the beginning of the end at Pearl Harbor, December 7, 1941. Almost four years had gone by, to be exact, from declaration of war December 8, 1941 to September 2, 1945 (three years, eight months, and 24 days). This war, on the Allies and Axis estimate, cost 40 million their lives, both military and civilians. In money, four trillion dollars. Through War II, 504, 245 lives have been lost in all USA wars. In War II, the US had 256,330 battle deaths. In War I, US casualties were 52,429. Our first war, the American Revolution, casualties were 4,435.

A very dark side of the war picture and of War II was the suicides. The Navy reported 174 officers and 473 enlisted men committed suicide. To this is added 93 Marines.

Epilogue—Sentinel Reunion

After almost 60 years since the sinking of the U.S.S. Sentinel, I set out to find any remaining survivors of that attack, in the hopes that I could connect with them as a gift to my grandfather for this 90th birthday. What transpired was an unforgettable journey. I wrote the following letter to Grandpa on December 22, 1999 to tell him of his surprise—it best tells the story of his Reunion:

Dear Grandpa:

You probably know by now what an important influence you have been on my life. I have lived 25 wonderful years under your care and support, and I am so thankful that we have been able to share so many wonderful memories—your visits to Austin when I lived there, cruises, and our unforgettable trip to Spain. I have also always been very interested in your experiences during World War II, and I wish I had a tape recorder to remember the many stories you have shared.

Your experiences in the War have always had a special place in my heart, and that has led to help you get your medals from the government, and more recently, the incredible photos of your ship. This interest has caused me to love all things about history and wars, and I feel somehow that I too am emotionally tied to your experiences.

I originally looked for pictures of your ship for your 90th birthday last summer, thinking that I would need that much time to find something. Little did I know how fast the pictures would arrive, and that left me with a desire to do a little more. So I decided to set out on a dream I have always wanted to do for you—to find your shipmates. What I didn't realize was that God had something far greater than my dream in store for this journey.

I got the Sentinel report from you a while ago listing your shipmates, and I have to admit that I was a little pessimistic about finding anyone. I called Veterans Affairs in Waco at the end of November, and I was connected to a lady named Gwen, who happily agreed to help. I faxed her the list of 81 enlisted survivors, and although she could not give me any current information on the phone, she agreed to mark out anyone who had unfortunately passed on, and then I could forward a letter to the remaining shipmates through VA. I immediately got excited when she quickly responded with the report that there are now 19 of the original 81 survivors still around!!!

I quickly prepared letters to send to these shipmates, not knowing what to expect. I received a response back from VA that out of the 18 letters I forwarded to them, they only had information for and forwarded letters to 10 shipmates.

What happened next was one of the most wonderful experiences of my life, and it has been so difficult keeping this news from you. I mailed the letters to VA on a Friday, VA received and forwarded the letters to the shipmates the following Monday, and I received my first phone call from one of your shipmates the next Thursday—Stanley Schley. He was very emotional on the phone and was extremely shocked to hear from me. He remembered you very well—he was a signalman (I think) who had a late-night shift. He says that you were like a father to him, since he was only 18 and you would constantly tell him to get some rest. He lives in Mission Hills, California, with his wife, and we talked for at least half an hour about the ship

70

and his life—it was so wonderful and weird to be hearing the same stories you tell from someone else.

I was shocked—I thought I might get a couple of letters or something—not phone calls. But maybe this was the one person who wanted to call and that would be it. Wrong! The very next day, I got a message at work and home from Edwin Deterge, who now lives in Los Angeles, California. He was 16 at the time of the War and is a coach at a local school. I returned his call the next day, Saturday morning, and we talked for a long while as he watched the Army-Navy game. Another emotional and wonderful experience.

I then started receiving letters and emails from other shipmates or their daughters—Arcue Grantland, Richard Everitt, George Blanton, and Edward Hutton - all very shocked and emotional about hearing from me - their correspondence is included with this letter. I also did some Internet research to find info on the eight men that I couldn't forward letters to. I looked up the names in a directory, and was able to find and contact two more men, George Flowers and Simon Michaluk. That was a totally different experience, because I wasn't even sure that they would be the right people, and I called them at home; you could imagine their surprise! So I have now had contact with eight men in all, nine including you, out of the available 19—not bad!!!

It's hard to describe the emotions I felt during this project. As I said earlier, I never realized what God had in store for me during this ordeal. I had always intended it to be for your benefit, but I looked past the fact that this would affect other people's lives as well. Daughters have written me thanking me for being able to learn more about their fathers. Shipmates have called each other already to talk. I then realized that God had used me as a catalyst for a bigger project, bigger than any one person could have imagined.

And finally, God has a message for you, too, and he gave it to me through this project. Almost all the men I have spoken to remember you very well. It would be safe to say that they remembered you more than anyone else, and that was because you helped them somehow—some in a big way during the bombing, some to bandage an ankle. Some said you saved their lives that day. After seeing this theme in almost every message I received, God seemed to speak to me this message—tell your grandfather to stop mourning the loss of the 10 men who died on the Sentinel, and rejoice in the 81 that lived, many with your help. I want you to see that there are men out there after all these years, with sons, daughters, grandsons, and granddaughters, and who lived wonderful, long lives.

I'm now going to read some of the letters I have received from your friends. One person, Stanley Schley, didn't want to write a letter—he wanted to see you in person. That is why he has agreed to come to the Sentinel reunion on Saturday, March 25th, your 90th birthday; hopefully others will be coming as well. I know you'll look forward to that wonderful day—Stanley was very excited when he called me recently to tell me he was coming.

Enjoy this collection of letters from your shipmates—it is a tribute to your life, your selflessness and servanthood that marks who you are to everyone who loves you. I love you and God Bless! I thought this verse was appropriate to end this letter ...

"For though we live in the world, we do not wage war as the world does. The weapons we fight with are not the weapons of the world. On the contrary, they have divine power to demolish strongholds." (2 Corinthians 10:3-4)

Grandpa did have his reunion in mid-March 2000. Four of his shipmates—Ed Anderson from Minnesota, Arcue Grantland from Florida, Charles La Gattuta from New York, and Simon Michaluk from Virginia flew in for the weekend. (Stanley Schley wasn't able to make it). Each shipmate brought a spouse, son, daughter, or friend, and it was as if we were having a family reunion with close relatives we hadn't seen in a very long time. We all instantly bonded, and the shipmates even more so.

My father contacted the local news networks and newspapers, and several stations arrived at my grandfather's 90th birthday party to cover the story. We sat the five shipmates in chairs in the middle of the party room, and camera lights flashed as if they were celebrities. And at the end of the party, the one thing my grandfather asked for was to lead the group in the Pledge of Allegiance.

It's no wonder they call his generation the greatest—it was only with men like my grandfather that we were able to live through such a harrowing time, and it was men like him that came back after the war to build a nation proud of its freedom and the sacrifice it takes to have it. This is my grandfather's story, but it's also the story of a generation.

GRANDPA (SECOND FROM LEFT)
WITH U.S.S. SENTINEL SHIPMATES, MARCH 2000

About the Authors

H.C. AND ADAM ON TOP OF THE ROCK OF GIBRALTAR, 1991

Hubbard Clements (H.C.) Goldsmith was born in 1910 in Lewisville, Texas. He served in the U.S. Navy in the early 1930s, and at the onset of World War II, served a second time from 1941 to 1945. He earned a Purple Heart for injuries sustained during his service in World War II. He died in 2000 in Dallas, Texas, and is buried at Arlington National Cemetary in Arlington, Viriginia.

Adam Gellert is H.C.'s grandson and an award-winning author. His book, "*Activation: A Story of God's Transforming Power*," won the 2016 Henri Christian Literary Award for Best Non-Fiction. He has a children's book in publication, as well as a book marketing guide. More information about Adam can be found at *AdamGellert.com*.